Milestones

Milestones

Poems selected by
Stephen Matthews

Milestones
ISBN 978 1 76109 166 7
Copyright © poems individual contributors 2021
Copyright © this selection Ginninderra Press 2021
Cover image: Brenda Eldridge

First published 2021 by
GINNINDERRA PRESS
PO Box 3461 Port Adelaide 5015
www.ginninderrapress.com.au

Contents

Introduction

Milestones was conceived as a vehicle to celebrate a year full of significant dates both personal (my 75th birthday, my son's 50th birthday) and professional (Ginninderra Press's 25th birthday). Australia Day 2021 brought with it the honour of an unexpected additional milestone – an Order of Australia Medal for service to publishing.

Within these pages, more than 160 Ginninderra Press poets explore their own take on milestones – personal and historical, mournful and whimsical, light and dark. To read the book from beginning to end is to take a poetic journey through the triumphs and setbacks, the heartache and joys of everyday life. I hope you'll enjoy reading *Milestones* and savour the diversity and insights within.

Stephen Matthews

Stepping Stones

Every poet's wildest dream a first book published
A whole world opens its arms
The smell of success wafts around
seeps into the consciousness of midnight waking hours
before fading somewhere
obliterated by the demands of everyday living

So ambition steps easily over the body of this achievement
Another book surely? The months pass
The next poems hide their differences
lining up obligingly in alphabetical order
in the computer documents file
before leaping into life in a more congenial order
in the pages of a second book

Even then a pinch   an itch remains
surviving the swell of praise and satisfaction
That blip on a far horizon seems tantalisingly accessible
the possibility of a third book – the ultimate prize
So now the crucial manuscript has been despatched
to await its turn in the maestro's long queue
A metabolic hibernation reigns
a longing for the ultimate milestone

Greg Tome

Emergence

Clamber up those rocks, he said. You will be able to see
where you have come from and the path ahead.
To clamber sounds soft, frolicsome, effortless.
Rocks I have known demanded that I heave myself
over their unforgiveness. I clamber, rasping breath and skin,
a toll for treading on silence. I stop at the top to wait
for a sense of arrival, for an urge to carve my name.
Is it beautiful? he calls.
I look at the spiky tufts of grass
the ones refusing to yield gracefully under my feet.
To the tree. Roots clinging to rocks like grasping hands.
With limbs twisted and crippled by elemental forces.
No, I call, it is not beautiful.
I don't mean where you are right now. His voice finds me
like a heat-seeking missile. I mean the panorama,
where you have come from and where you are going.
I let his words float past me.
I sit under the tree, beside the grass.
Cashmere air wraps around us. A trio of survivors.
Together we breathe and pulse in silent rhythm.
His voice insists. Can you see how far you are travelling?
That it's a milestone for you?
No, I shout. Yes, I whisper, without arrow or marker I know
I have arrived.

Judy Rafferty

The final destination

Sentinels by the roadside, of concrete or of wood,
Silent they stand and tell us the miles as they should;
And if by chance a letter is shown,
The destination will clearly be known.

My own milestones are nothing like the road's,
They have their own rhythms, their very own modes.
Birthdays, of course, are known in advance,
But all other milestones are subject to chance.

My first day of school and, years later, my last,
My first kiss, a love affair that's now way in the past.
A licence, a second-hand car, and driving's allowed;
Graduation, my first pay cheque, I'm ever so proud.

My wedding, the first child, a second, but two is enough,
The death of a parent, or of a friend; times can be tough.
The children move out, my career comes to an end,
The twilight years have arrived, years of a special blend.

These are my milestones, the ones that I know.
There've been many of them and one more to go.
Destination is clear, is acknowledged and known,
But the distance, the distance is simply not shown.

Margitta Acker

E becomes L

We all follow unseen signs
as we trundle through life,
first in pram, and later Zimmered.
There's one pointing the way
to dusty school, and some of us stay
far too long, that sign states
exactly how many years our eyes
will strain themselves over books,
but we're too engrossed to read it.
There are signs for romance,
signs for kids, signs for jobs,
marking forty years for many.
Forty years dividing the day
into sandwiches of time,
until we picnic on superannuation,
knees creaking as we spread the rug.
And of course, there's the last sign
we avoid reading; the millstone
always tied to our feet, our brain,
the final milestone buried out of sight.
We put up a sign after that event
(or relatives do) saying who we were.
And then worms write us up
with their wriggly calligraphy,
signing off on our flesh with glee.

PS Cottier

Earth Therapy

In every forest there's a dance and song,
the embouchure of breeze awakens trees –
picnicers sense this silent concert; free
of tickets, dress codes and all that is wrong
with a world hard, angular; circles gone
that once were pond and bush. So here we breathe
in life's drug, taste the wine of truth and see,
for an afternoon, the moss and leaves, shone
with water's mirrored light. But when four walls
surround city souls and the only rocks
are gravel and stolen boulders, there falls
a sick pallor. Shackles of routine lock
us inside heads and homes. So, drown the rules.
Milestones don't tick to conformity's clock.

Jude Aquilina

Step by Step

Wondering, meditating
on my next step to success.
I think of ancient Romans years ago
counting all those thousand paces
as they marched through history.

Will I achieve my goal, my milestone,
as they did?
Why sit still when I can have a go,
striving to meet success?

We achieve the impossible when we have a go.
I had to start anew, months
till I could learn to write again.

Many steps along my path:
life's significant steps.
Milestones consume the story of my life
sparking progress.

A celebration of memorable moments
and momentous milestones.
Accompanied by music,
my exuberant song of victory rings out.

Airlie Jane Kirkham

Ad Astra Per Aspera

Perfect late afternoon. The inner voice whispers,
'Don't question. Go for a walk to Sparrow Reserve.'

Do. Sit on a bench, remembering where, a life time ago,
I sat on the way to Woodville High School. I was 17.
Back then, the inner voice rang clear,
'You will be a director.'
Of what? Turned out to be a theatre director.
Still am, all these years later.

I remembered the teacher who said, 'You're thick.
Not creative. Book-keeping's for you.'
Zombied in an accounting office
for seven years until suddenly quitting, walking out,
into, you guessed it. Theatre directing,

Milestone moments remembered. Returned home.
On the way an old man shuffling with a cane.
When will this be me?

Past. Present. A future yet to come.
Ad Astra Per Aspera.
Still reaching for the stars, with difficulty.

Martin Christmas

Milestone millstone

A new study, by Pedro Loans, has revealed there are 25 milestones which we should all be aspiring to. – *Belfast Telegraph*

Apparently:
By age 15 I should have had my first kiss.
> *Nup, fail. Was 19 before that happened.*

By age 20 I should have my drivers licence.
> *Bewdy, back on schedule!*
> *Four late and four early makes me even!*

By age 30 be settling down. Life-partner, mortgage and car.
> *Two out of three ain't bad.*

By age 35 have first child.
> *Oh, the one I missed is bad after all.*
> *Unless there's something I don't know.*

By age 36 take an overseas holiday.
By age 38 buy a holiday house.
By age 40 become a manager at work, buy
an investment property, or start my own consultancy.
No.

Sorry, I'm sick of this.
These materialistic ideals
are not mine.

Hmm. You don't suppose a loan company would
have an ulterior motive in making me aspire to this
do you?

Russ Talbot

Stones That Mark a Passage

Are these pebbles that indicate the *mani* path?
More likely you get boulders
to keep you on the rolling belt:
gift of Christmas before the New Start,
birthdays, weekends, sport and film fandom.
Where job-wife-kids-career mean home –
along with seven ages of man, flu jabs,
taxes – and maxims in a cracker.
But how does all *that* – incorporate:
learning to walk three times before you are 14,
never sniffling but hospitalisation for the Big Hits,
the exile from people to harsh, open spaces,
making last dwelling payment a month after severance,
being hurt then learning to hurt, at love.

You only decide to fly
by finding your balcony.
You can get to there by finally staying here.
And now the final milestone approaches…
There's nothing left to explain but hope.

Danny Gardner

Mani path refers to the system of Nepalese trade trails around
Everest with its mani stones as a guide (you always keep them on
your right).

The Passage of Time

The passage of time
is marked by milestones
unescapable
through the journey of life
sometimes insignificant
yet often remarkable
unbelievable

sometimes seemingly
impossible to achieve
yet hope sustains us
as a milestone beckons
and keeps us alive
as we strive to reach it
bringing such delight

An unexpected happenstance
can bring joy with
the pleasure
of a milestone long awaited
yet unexpected
as we pass along
in the passage of time

Edna Taylor

Milestoned

Insecure to the brim
Pathetically so
Swamping achievements
And moments of mirth
Till I'm counting the dark clouds
Instead of marking milestones.

An unsettled foundation
Creates an unstable structure
A disquieted brain
Can't silence itself.

While some would (and do) celebrate
I'm occupied spying obstacles
Before they arise.

Perhaps milestones are best
Marked by others
To remind us
Where we've been
As some of us
Can't visualise the sky
Beyond the storm.

Anthony J. Langford

Upward Stride

I gazed over titanium beach
the headland so far out of reach.
I ran along with springing stride
beside the sparkling, rippling tide.

A voice called me from on high
as dunes reached toward the sky
Run this way, it seemed to say
This is your path, come what may.

I turned, began to run upslope
my arms swinging with all good hope
my feet sank into grainy sand
how I needed a helping hand.

Rocket plants and spiky mounds
marked my straining muscle bounds
The voice said, 'You're at the crest.'
Life led me up, now time to rest.

Looking far across the bay
it was here I longed to stay.
The voice said, 'More peaks ahead.'
So down and up again I tread.

Geoff Graetz

Point Zero

Keystone for a ragtag straggle of a prison,
the obelisk stands: to measure is to control.
Macquarie's doomed vision – yeoman farms,
dominion imposed in rod perch or pole,

inscribed origin of the outward push –
Windsor, Bathurst, Parramatta,
its stone hacked from a stubborn land,
Greenway's design to decree and flatter:

it proclaimed the radiating roads,
erased the sympathetic songlines,
dreamtime links to sacred sites,
overlaid an ancient map's arcane signs.

Incongruous relic in its inner city park,
visible then from the whole fragile settlement,
now, with companion anchor and cannon,
a quaint curiosity no longer eminent.

Now it's smothered in unseasonal smoke
and on the heirs a new fear descends,
the limits of control become apparent,
the land threatens a measure of revenge.

Geoff Lucas

Stone Miles

There were stones beside the highway, carved, setting forth
new distances in Imperial measure from a starting point
a metaphor to begin then tangible it too emerging from stone
the Obelisk, standing, in bold recognition of its Governor.

Sand stones carved and embedded beside the Great Western
enumerated in Roman all the way to who knows where now
certainly not Bathurst, nor Mt Victoria, not even Penrith
where once thirty-five stood as rough ashlars counting down

The Great Road between Civilisation and a bold Frontier.
Give Mr Cox the task they said and the Governor in his infinite
wisdom did with the same sense of occasion anoint Mr Cureton
carver of milestones, and obelisks, and dwarf stone walls.

I remember as a small child seeing them from the back seat
of the grey Morris Minor in barren landscape till neon from
Broadway breweries lit my imagination beyond apprehension
all thoughts of straight great roads falling backward forever

Now the milestones are gone, the Imperial is a faded memory.
To travel the great Mr Cox's road from Mr Cureton's Obelisk
through Parramatta and on to Penrith requires nothing more
than to listen to satellite navigators with Chinese accents.

Richard Stanton

The Fifty-mile Mark

Once, they placed this arch-shaped stone to mark
A time in space, rough-hewn, a distance known
Entombed in crumbling sandstone, stark
Now chiselled by deluge rain, and dark
Now pulled down by the ancient loam
'Fifty miles from here, and you'll be there', a sentinel
That stood, once tall for all to read
Once passed by drays in rutted clay, yet clear to see.

Now the turf has sucked beneath our tread,
In turn of time,
A flicker thought passed through my mind,
As blindly we were driven past and steered
By smooth concrete now, by shining steel, here
A simple stone once stood, still and clear

And rain released that scent of wild, and real.
When distance was something strange, unclear,
And time, inured by past deeds now averred,
For us, the past, a mere child, age interred.

Chris Hall

Reset

Entangled, skewed, forgotten
a chiselled sandstone slab
stands. Its former status
yields to concrete lanes of progress.

Out around this ten-mile
visions were hewn, gauged, discarded.
Maybe not all!
Tangled in memory, a choice endures.

Welcome it.
Listen for its venerable voice
scour its layered patina
allow it to reset your journey.

Michael Keating

Lighting the Way

Milestones announce the distance to a place I've never been
thereby counting miles I've covered from the start
Sometimes when a milestone flares in reflected light
I shiver
not all stones hold warmth
Through half-closed eyes I can almost see early milestones
faded flickering wicks of time trapped behind old sunsets
Markers I have hurried past are left forever unsaluted,
untended, smothered now by undergrowth
while way back near this road's beginning
four cold stones lie underwater
flooded and rubbed smooth
by waterfalls of tears

I look ahead at milestones not yet read
they don't mark time or heartbeat
they don't mark hills and swamps and sinkholes
between me and the place I've never been
so I will stop at each remaining one
feel its heat, find its shade
touch every mile that's left to travel
and if I look back and the road is dark
I'll smile at you and hope you'll smile for me

Joanne Ruppin

5 Miles to London

Once I was a rolling stone, free and on the move, until someone, decided to put me to work. Gave me a place in history, as it were. Measured up, I became gainfully employed directing traffic. This was all eons ago, when I was shapely, smooth and white. In those days, everyone was heading for London. People, men on horseback, coaches and drays all stopped, relied on my accurate directions. Everything changed as the city grew. Eventually, progress brought a by-pass on the old road.

So, I stand here, a marker on life's forgotten highway. Go on pointing the way. The way to nowhere. Years pass and no one has come searching for me. Nobody realises my true worth. Abandoned, I have become an anachronism, not a memorial. Mistakes have been made, fake stones heralded, set up in my place. I know I'm well past my use-by date, but in the future, who will even remember the song, the story of Dick Wittington? Who will know that, tired and dejected, he sat right here, five miles from London? Heard the Bow Bells calling him back to his master, his cat. And a memorable life.

Brenda Saunders

My Birthday

At both ends
of the main street
roundabouts.

At one
the road north
to Sydney.

The other
is the road south
to Berry.

At one there is no milepost.
The survivor is so eroded
by rain and wind and weather

that it cannot be read,
a worn monolith
in yellow sandstone,

neither functional
nor decorative
but still, solidly there.

John Egan

Halfway

It stands, incongruous beside the garden barbecue,
a piece of bygone age thrust up from earth
to challenge me, my space
my time, my age, my comfort zone.
A solid post, River Gum
now old and grey. One face
towards the south – M 6
the northern face – H 7
Halfway from somewhere on the road to – where?
6 feet long 10 inches square
Somehow seems more comfortable
to keep to feet and inches.
Half buried, half above the earth,
its message there for weary travellers.
Numbers clear, straight, hand-carved.
It speaks a time when you could see
man's hand skills on display,
saw marks, chisel cuts.
It has a presence, even pride.
I sit here with my coffee,
enjoy, meditate, give thanks
that this old craftsman's skills
are here for me to contemplate.

David Harris

Ship's Library

An unknown traveller has marked
this poem in a five-hundred
poem book, signalling boldly

a change of course, storm-driven
a coming alongside, a mooring
a lighthouse seen after months

of rudderless drift, foam wakes.
An unknown traveller has found
their anchor poem here

all others cast over
mere ballast between shores
four thousand miles apart.

Ann Nadge

Living My Way

My family were aghast as I loved books too well.
I was under a magic spell cast by words,
Not by a witch in the dark woods.
I saw life mirrored in stories of others and in books.
Like in stories I could win against the odds.
By now I have passed many signposts, sometimes in cars
That had seen better days like cats with nine lives.
One job was solitary in an office in winter,
Desolate, skeletal trees all around
Pointing twisted fingers at the sky.
A hawk drove a hapless bird against the outer wall
With a deafening thud before flying away.
The prey fell like a stone soon stiff like a stick in death.
My tiny car was pursued by big trucks on the way,
A symbol of how some people are rapacious as hawks.
They stalk words like predators stalking prey,
Waiting for a missed word, a pause, a typo;
Waiting for me to go away, like assassins,
Or like people going berserk with road rage.
They fear my words might lead me or them astray.
Now I feel I have achieved much,
Just by surviving to tell my stories my way.

Adriana Wood

The gradually disappearing bookshop

for Kris and Loretta Hemensley and Collected Works Bookshop

Eye of Horus
Hand of God
Protect and bless
This bookshop
This inevitably
Vanishing bookshop.
Bless and protect
All who sailed in her
And its captains.
O my captains!
Sally forth
With your books
Aloft. A loft
In a cottage
In Northcote.
Hand of God.
Eye of Horus.

Ray Liversidge

Stained glass window on the past

Candleflame and coloured glass
shine and remind us both tonight
of an old religion's ways, long lost:
the bluestone church with altar, hymns,
prayers for unacknowledged sins.

Here, the household gods assemble now:
roses float in the blue glass bowl
on a linen cloth laid down for our meal;
the candle's flickering halo of light
colours two who lean in and laugh.

Suzanne Edgar

The Church Organ

Every Sunday, the old church organ sang
in tune with the choir,
her mellow voice resonating
through the high-ceilinged chamber,
vibrating against polished wood and stained glass

Her ivory keys lovingly caressed
by a parade of hands,
some young and plump, some weathered and bent,
yet all respectful of her age and breeding

But time spiralled and years passed
and the old church organ
became an antique – a curiosity,
inevitably replaced by iPod and speakers,
their notes crisp and clear
but no match for her full-bodied voice.

Now, no longer singing with the Sunday choir,
still she has her part to play,
cosily ensconced behind glass
in the local museum, her keys now silenced.
But her song lives on in the hearts of those who remember

Colleen Moyne

Mary Wollstonecraft, September 1797

The labour is hard and long, but finally you produce
a frail and puny child – a daughter, who'll later dance
with poets and at age nineteen create a monster she names
Frankenstein. 'Tis a pity – you're not to know. For you've
only ten days more to live. Your bed will shake with your
trembling, pain screaming jets of blood. Inside you, festering
fragments of afterbirth will do unfettered work. Invisible.
Murderous. Your intelligence and eloquence will haemorrhage
out when, placed upon your engorged breasts, tiny puppies
begin to suckle there and thus draw out your milk.
An eighteenth-century grotesquerie to be sure.
Defiled, debased, distressed, your rational mind will reel.
So much for the *Rights of Women and the Perfectibility
of Man.* There'll be no Reason in your bedchamber. But you
know the signs. You've seen how Reason can go mad. Back when
black despair darkened the sunny skies of hope, when tumbrils
rumbled over cobblestones and the blood-soaked blade of
the guillotine fell on the deadly drumbeats of the Reign of Terror.
No commemorations or honouring then. Nor any now for you.
No dignity either – just the stench of bloodied bedsheets
and a sullied reputation for being you.

Had you but known your life, your work would one day become
a milestone, a blazing beacon of inspiration for all womankind,
would you have smiled?

Roslyn McFarland

Letter to Theo

Vincent Van Gogh: *Starry Night Over the Rhône*, 1888

The evening stunned my senses. Showers of stars
outlined in indigo, as bright as day,
above the Rhône in gold and chartreuse rays
transfixed it with empyrean repertoire.
It must have been quiescence of the Bear
that coaxed me from inside my solitude
into the star-scape's strange infinitude
of constellations in the gaslight's glare.
As if heaven itself had magnified the spheres,
to drown my stubborn spirit in its light,
releasing myriads of stalactites.
I stood there mute. Then noticed, on the pier,
two young lovers, blind to all that grace.
So I spilled the stars on canvas. Just in case.

Hazel Hall

The icon

On viewing The Bridge in Curve *by Grace Cossington Smith*

The wished-for sun slides through
the sheet of true-blue sky

spotlights the bridge,
halves of its span still under construction,

not yet met.
It's all about the hopeful

coupling of virgin arcs suspended, impossibly
in the sky,

faith ascending, tense excitement
of a first illicit kiss.

Linda Albertson

Humour in the face of it

Lives on rations and hopes kept in bounds.
No shortages, though, on the lists of the missing
nor rumours of jackbooted plunder.
From a bested war office a desperate edict:
Topple the signposts, uproot the milestones,
make nameless your village, your stations and churches.
Whatever you can to confuse the invaders.
And keep the Good Lord with you all.

*

Came a grinding, an ominous grumbling of half-tracks.
Old men reliving their previous wars.
Breaths held. Arms embracing. Children made silent.
Mishearing each sound as the dread tread of soldiers.

*

But the dangers came not from pillaging foe.
The early invaders were Aussies and Yanks
Jammed tightly in hedgerows, maps spread over bonnets.
Comrades in arms nearly coming to blows.

*

Contrary directions from laconic locals
wryly quoting 'The Grand Old Duke…'
as they lean on uprooted milestones.

Colin Rogers

Special Edition

National holiday. Conga lines, dancing in Piccadilly
Circus and Pall Mall. Street parties, bunting,
royals wave from balcony – seven times.

Shouts, cheers, hugs, waltzing in towns
all over Britain. Couples kiss at the top
of lampposts. Churchill's victory speech,

unconditional surrender. Rule Britannia,
Britannia rules the waves. Spotlight on
St Paul's. Cathedrals, symbol

of resistance. Our boys free to return
home. Thank God it's over. A shiver
for our sons who didn't make it.

We'll meet again one fine day. Her eyes blur,
lump in throat, squeeze hands, silent prayer. A
whisper,
it's more like a funeral than sacred jubilation.

Nazi Party emblem shot away. Church bells
chime, the first time since 1940. VE Day, one
of the greatest celebrations in history.

Decima Wraxall

The digital utopian: in memory of Richard Brautigan

'Information is the future,' he said, conjuring
pastoral grace from the industrial real –
deer and humans tended by machines,
cybernetic meadows, Richard swinging
in a hammock, spinning words
in a summer of love. Later, channelling
Hemingway, he crafted a .44 calibre
bullet hole in his head. No more trout-fishing
in America, the dream elusive
as the trout itself, no back-to-nature
at Bolinas, no poets lounging in long grass.
Only a frog, once, snatched and eaten
from a windowsill, a last mad gesture
when all else seemed lost, the harmonious
'has to be' faded: no more questions
to field as dark descended. And for us?
Not so far off, no fish, no mammals, no water.
If sky, then livid streaks like Mexican fire opal.
No grace remains when polar bears drift by
on infinitely calving icebergs, when the last
mammal and final us lie stiff and glass-eyed
and strangely companionable in some
cobweb-corner of a dust-bowl planet.

Louise Wakeling

Reducing the Tyranny of Distance

Famously, in 1974,
When miles shrank to kilometres
And metrication spread like a mist,
One jest was popularly repeated:

'Give him 2.54 centimetres
And he'll take 1.61 kilometres' –
While Sydney rattlers still passed the sign
Griffiths Teas 5 Miles.

But highway milestones soon disappeared
Only to reappear in front gardens
Announcing 17 miles to Wagga Wagga,
Even though this was now from Batemans Bay.

Something comforting was conveyed
Beside the garden gnomes and hydrangea
And a white-painted tyre surrounding
A poinsettia or Christmas bush.

By such reductions in scale
The Great Australian Distance was soothingly
Reduced, as in the case of Wollongong
Being three miles from Broken Hill.

John Watson

Late in the Evening

Central Park, that September evening of 1981;
the heart of New York pulsed to the beat of a generation.
The songwriter and the voice
together again for one last concert;
and how they played,
how they rocked their native New York City,
played on into the night
to a crowd who'd arrived before daybreak
and waited all day,
hanging on a momentous reunion.
For seventy-five minutes they let go their differences,
built a bridge over their troubled waters,
sang of Mrs Robinson, of the boxer
and of Julio down by the schoolyard,
sang to a crowd intoxicated,
who echoed back the lyrics to every song.
Two iconic figures, silhouettes against the skyline
as daylight dimmed and darkness settled
minute by minute on the park; the audience still swaying,
singing every well-known word
just a little less loud as
the night wore on,
blown away by the performance
that marked the end of an era.

Margaret Zanardo

Shoemaker's Moon

And, when he shall die
Take him and cut him out in little stars
And he will make the face of heaven so fine
That all the world will be in love with night
And pay no worship to the garish sun.

Shakespeare, *Romeo & Juliet*

He'd trained as an astronaut for the moon,
disqualified by a doctor's report,
there on the surface, his ashes were strewn.

From Addison's Curse, he wasn't immune,
he'd tracked eight hundred asteroids: his art,
and trained as an astronaut for the moon.

He died in Australia, much too soon,
exploring a crater, his life cut short,
there on the surface, his ashes were strewn.

Eugene Shoemaker, that cold afternoon,
was left alone in the regolith dirt,
he'd trained as an astronaut for the moon.

Lunar Prospector carried the tomb
of Shoemaker's remains, on the transport,
there on the surface, his ashes were strewn.

A quote from Shakespeare was etched on his ruins,
a wife and three daughters, mourning and hurt,
he'd trained as an astronaut for the moon
there on the surface, his ashes were strewn.

Joe Dolce

Unsettled

Old man, have you lost your way
skin on bone through stained clothes
slumped over polished table under lantern glow
wandering your street and local haunts
now cafés bars fine restaurants

Old man, have they lost their way
poised promises, they come they go
occupation liberation dispossession dissipation
through your milestone malaise
nameless streets evolve faceless cities
mankind left the moon and towers split the ground
as laser lights brighten waterfalls

Old man, have we lost our way
flight or fight grips tight as we stare elsewhere
what disillusionment gazing through our wine
my thought-samaritan in overdrive as we sit and dine
where is your family how can we help
   don't interfere…locals don't

Old man, have I found my way
decades gone…your image still lingers

Donna Edwards

47

Felling Trees and Other Turning Points

At a wake for a cousin in a country town

We drove around the oval, saw the old grandstand –
so small and cute, behind Granny's large estate,
just as I remembered it when I was four,
a playground for us cousins
playing tricks on each other.
But over there, the pine trees told
a different story – a cutting of limbs.
My uncle was felled by one,
doing a service for the community,
and his teenage son saw it all – and then
his brother took his life.
What a demolition was that,
what an uprooting of a family's life.

But some turning points are positive.
In the 50s, in a Housing Trust area,
one had to bear the neighbours' views.
When, after year 11, I was offered a job
by the local bank manager – we never went there
by the way – no money, no car – my mother
resisted the offer, earning their scorn and disgust.
'You're up yourself,' they said.
'She's only a girl and you need the money.'
She sent me on, with five brothers,
to higher schooling, giving me what she
had been denied, against the tide of the times.

Ros Schulz

Treating Me as an Old Growth Tree

dendrochronology (n.) linking history to age rings in trees

You dendro-pathologists charting rates of tree growth,
harvest my year rings with hollowed-out drill bits,
storing samples to compare in dry paper straws.
From there, do your testing on scars in my bark sheath
still damp with moss on the south side of eyeballs,
where bags are now sagging to a shed-skin degree.
Do not hesitate to leech my most anaemic of blood sap,
as you bore your way into a deciduous dermatology
to calibrate a graphing of hazards to health,
drilling through age-rings laid close as drought growth,
auguring out hardwood turned soft by dry rot…

But never be loath to lop my lowest branches
if you reckon I'm rooted – too deep in my subsoil –
after being seen as shiftless by some whilst a sapling.
For light years I have photosynthesised wider age arcs,
intent on making up for seasons left fruitless,
till your tree surgeon colleague cut through one key limb
with a power saw, replacing a knee with nyloned titanium.
Too ingrained in my ways – despite blue-sky leaf shoots –
to shift ground with ease, given the depth of my taproot,
I hold tight here as summer threatens forest fire scarring,
now my seed growth is safe in an urban plantation.

Rodney Williams

At the Roadside on Skye

Leaving the sealed air of the driver's side and getting out
onto heath, I took the full brunt of the wind and heights
to stand braced beside a lichened milestone, its angled
granite protrusion like a piece of the earth's bone
broken through the skin. What broke through me, then,
come far from my source, taking my reckoning?
The milestone's rough confronting; its name trying out
the memory; like capstone, lodestone, grindstone, words
to break your teeth on, meanings heavy on the tongue.
The whetstone from my father's garage bench, the hard
scrape along its oblong as he honed a chisel blade
to come keen and glinting as a horizon line. The home
hearthstone under a blaze of coals where I was forged
and shaped and drawn from. And now the milestone's
weathered markings, betraying origins or further distances,
my eyes smarting to imprint; like when I took rubbings
off a windblown gravestone, half a world away;
the dates' faint inscription; another journey line
and halt. Wherever I am, I am a brief fixed point
in blustering air, trying to get a bearing, still everything
quickly heading on; as above that roadside, a small bird,
triumphing in the blasts, wheeled and circled overhead,
travelling its course in rounds, like a winged heart,
always coming back to where it started.

Philip Radmall

Returning To Eden

(now an island)

No wings to fly or boat to cross fishy moat
so bridge of words. Strait too rough,
too cold to swim. Easier ways to stimulate
heart than climb the mountainous, merciless.
Where does that leave me, besides on
wrong side of whatever water is?
Mad moves don't make choreography.

The more I think about it, the more I think
about it and the more becoming it becomes.
Why actually go there, considering stress,
packing/unpacking, neighbours' noisy dogs.
(That may have seemed like it should end
with question mark.) Bridge is wish,
is flying horse, is poem that can span.

Once there I can stop dwelling on return
to Cradle, listen to a waterfall, gorge
on original fruit. Places to revisit long,
yet to visit longer. Lone pilgrimage.
It'll take what remains of me and then
the remains of me. Still, there will be
shy mountains, ferny gullies, wise witness
eucalypts, deserted stone beaches that lull
with indecipherable code and offer
a welcoming emptiness.
My unlikely return long overdue –
apple, snake and always you.

Allan Lake

haiku

milestone
another flaming arrow
misses me

Judith E.P. Johnson

Summation

A date of birth
A date of death

A small dash between

The dash the summation of a life

Did she plod slowly
through her ninety-five years?

Did he run helter-skelter
through a short life but a merry one?

Did they spread joy and laughter
gifting others with wisdom?

We live our own eulogies

How will your eulogist answer the question

'What did you do with your dash?'

Brenda Eldridge

An X-ray in 1966

The cottage hospital is strangely quiet,
one other patient in the waiting room,
only one nurse in Radiology.

'I'm not busy here today,' she says.
'I'll get the plate developed right away
so that you can see it for yourself.'

It's not exactly unexpected news
but still a shock. I know from this day on
nothing will ever be the same again.

I leave the building, start my journey home
with growing panic prowling through my mind.
I feel my eyes fill up and overflow.

A woman at the bus stop sees my face
and asks me kindly, 'Have you had bad news?'
She offers me a friendly handkerchief.

I dab my eyes and summon up a smile.
I hand the hankie back to her and say,
'No, I've just found out I'm having twins.'

Mary Jones

Move, Baby!

Felt the first flutterings yesterday,
From deep inside my belly's billowing
A tiny sea-horse weaving on its way,
Hard to believe it's thirteen inches now!
Rollicking gently through the liquid sky,
Then, mermaids dancing and horses prancing
On frothing waves when winds kick up the spray
Getting more strenuous as the days go by.
I'm now my baby's coffer, keeper, den
Wherein she plays upside down with tiny feet
And walks upon my cage like Jonah in the whale
I wonder if I can sneeze her out, now that she's whole?
From beauteous mortals we require enhance
It's part of a greater portrait – a game of chance.

Anne Skyvington

First Child

First quiet thought
First whispered wish thickening
First nausea
First beating heart quickening

First timid arms around
Unsuspecting father
First disbelief and
Faltering fearful wonder

First kick beneath the skin
First tumble within

First clench
First bending, moaning wrench
First gathering screaming gasp
First crying painful laugh

First wakening breath
First opened eyes and finger grasp
First sudden fierce love
First quiet terror blast

Tracey-Anne Forbes

Connection

A newborn placed upon the mother's breast
first touch of hands relieves the pain of birth
and skin on skin, the urgent wait for breath.

A moody world, the fight to live – first breath
the union where the chimes expand the breast,
ring out the cry of life, the toll of birth.

A love that touches, knows this heart, this birth
and pleasure draws each day the perfect breath
connects the cave of love within the breast.

The breast, our birth, the breath, spent force – then death.

Helene Castles

Skin to Skin

A new head nestled
by your neck, the love
of your daughter's labour
to cup with your hand;
her hair a light sheen, her
slow milky sighs, her body
huddled into your chest.

And mid-century say,
may corals bloom and rains
lull, and the winds soothe
her face; and may she lie
skin to skin with her other
on the earth we've willed
to hold and brim with life.

Kathryn Fry

New Arrival

You've arrived!
Bursting
with the cry of all humanity
into the relentless light.
You continue us,
a prediction of the future.
We expected you,
anticipated, prepared,
but still
a long breath, a sigh,
and tiny muscles stitch this wild-eyed day.
Welcome, O welcome.

John Weerden

A Christening Wish

For you, my grandson, I wish
forests full of birds and bats
and spiders big as daddy's hats,
squid and octopus squirting ink,
streams where lizards come to drink,
fat wombats and bouncing roos
and beach to walk without your shoes,
bees that buzz for hours and hours
making honey from the flowers.

I wish for you
wild places where wild boys can play
and fish and hide and run all day,
rainforest where possums swing
and bush where little spinebills sing,
coral reefs, crocs and billabongs,
seals and whales and wobbegongs,
sunshine, rain and windy weather
and wilderness
that goes on
forever.

Brendan Doyle

too late

outside the nursing home
I think it's May
let's just say it's May

surrounded by my husband's family
– well not all of them –
as we take a break
from the deathbed vigil

sleep-deprived and exhausted
from night feeds and nappy changes
I'm half listening, half tuning out
the river of words murmuring around me
and breaking on the rocks of what
we are not saying

I look away for the briefest moment
and everyone exclaims
laughs
as she takes her first steps
I turn, but I am too late

Indrani Perera

Starting School

(Past and present difficulties)

I've woken singing Mrs D,
Mrs I, Mrs FFI,
Mrs C, Mrs ULT
And can't get it out of my mind.

It was the way in grade 1a
They taught us how to spell, and where
Trauma from playground bullying
Meant I learnt little more than this

Word and had to repeat the class,
Endure my younger brother there,
The shame of him having not just
Caught up but also coming first

While I was still listed as last,
The jealousy that wrecked love for
Him ever growing, and now this
Chant maddening, rubbing it in.

Graeme Hetherington

Astrakhan

a Russian childhood

When you speak of Astrakhan,
images detach from time,
a window saturates with light
as scenes from childhood flood the mind.

You hold a spoon where droplets glow
like gems in wisps of autumn breath;
past windows mirrored in your eyes
the cranes migrate, a white horse glides.

At dusk, his shadow-neck and mane
are stained Rose Madder, amethyst,
as waterfowl cry fretful from the river-
verge and old men fish.

Gazing from the water's edge,
the far shore hidden from your sight,
the Volga seems as infinite
and lonely as the winter skies.

Jena Woodhouse

The magpie

The lone magpie comes to the bottlebrush
        new-flowering in my yard

chooses a branch and perches,
        head moving cannily from side to side,

beak rhythmically rubbing the bark.
        It is so quiet I hear its thoughts;

but when it sings, it's dancing dragonflies
        and water warbling over rocks,

willows whispering secrets to the river
        near scorched summer paddocks.

It's children's voices as they splash in shallows –
        the *quardle oodle wardle* of their joy.

Pip Griffin

Words in italics are from 'The Magpies' by Denis Glover

Portrait of two-year-old with tired mother

She squats,
absorbed,
in the middle of the road.

Mother halts, ten paces ahead.
Eases her many-bag burdens.

What now? We're almost home.

Sun-brown child raises her eyes,
reluctant to look away from the black road –
a splotch of engine oil
has met and mingled with the morning rain.

Rainbow fell down

Voice intent, she must
share this miracle with her mother.

Look   rainbow fell down

Her first metaphor –

rainbow fell down.

Gina Mercer

Memory's territory

10 years old
on my King of the Road scooter.
Its red enamel frame
and white, pneumatic tyres
absorbed most shocks
as I zoomed from the local shops
down childhood's winding path.

Adolescent on a skateboard
with orange deck
and green, translucent wheels.

I took exquisite risks
then safely slowed down
using driveways like
runaway truck ramps,
and came to a stop
outside my house.

Those worlds, now extinct,
were entirely of my making.
Dangerous and free.
Memory's territory.

Mark Mahemoff

Memory From Childhood

I'd seen it done before to 'Jingle Bells'
two empty beer bottles with
spoons sitting upside down in the top
shaken to the rhythm
then clinked together at Hey!
and I'm transported
but I go beyond control
don't know about restraint
I love the sensation, the sound
the smell of the dregs
and my excitement bolts
until all holdback is gone
and on the next clink
my joy breaks with
the shatter and spray of brown glass
the tinkle of spoons on concrete
my father's gentle voice as I surrender what's left
two bottle necks
two spoons
my embarrassment.

Fran Graham

Blood Calendar

On the first day of becoming a woman
her father called the doctor
for appendicitis, or some such bodily malfunction
but it was only the ache of delivering
the first of many unfertilised beings.

After the time of deflowering
she expected to find a proud stain on the sheet—
a mark of the milestone to womanhood. Yet
no evidence was found in blood, or esteem.

When at last a missed cycle signalled conception
she forgave all the monthly suffering.
Her brother sent claret roses. She rode a wave of belonging
to the whole ebb and flow of the universal scheme.
But her man reassured that she wasn't to blame when
the blood returned too soon. He planted seeds of rosemary.

And when in time her river ran dry
she had relief from the cyclic cry though nothing
to show for the years of fruitless labouring.

On the first day of becoming a woman
her father gave her a posy of wild violets. Delicate. Sweet.
(Yet strange to be congratulated for an involuntary feat?)
Decades later, the bouquet was still pressed and sealed, to
mark the inaugural blood event – a purple heart of courage
for the many years spent
fighting silent wars on invisible battlefields.

Melissa Bruce

First School Social

I wore a red dress, woollen fabric trimmed in gold
sewn with meticulous care by my mother
Looks like a flannel nightgown, said my brother
older than me but had never been to a social

I walked the dark mile to school in my flat black shoes
Too scared to stand like a horse at an auction
waiting for a bid, I hid behind a pillar
to avoid the dark gangling boy
who reminded me of a tarantula

My only dance partner was the maths teacher
Of the three girls in the class he had a crush on one
To allay suspicion he danced with all three

Teachers roamed the ground with torches
while I crept around the dance floor
in the shadows of the bold

Jennifer Chrystie

The First Time

I was fourteen.
You were older.
We were at
a daytime screening
of *A Hard Day's Night*.
It was Saturday afternoon
nineteen-sixty-something.

Your elbow
nudged my elbow.
Your thumb
stroked the back of my hand.
My palm
turned to meet yours.
Our fingers
interlinked.

More memorable
than any kiss;
so much better
than sex.

I still remember
that first time.

Judy Dally

Pandemic journeys…becoming a longhair

An unexpected journey to the past
when crew to college cut
gave way to growing hair.
Not Beatle moptop or Surfie peroxide blonde,
no Sobranie black Russian cigarettes,
nor burgundy cord coat nor Herman Hesse books,
not a 'Kulcha Bugger', the other kind of 'longhair'.

Now, could side hair growth,
please forget the centre,
confer distinction or even wisdom,
or an older Carlton Left intellectual persona?

'Give me a head with hair…long, beautiful hair…'
Assiduously avoiding the hairdresser's wagging finger,
the hairs grew, even many of them.
Had I acquired a dignified leonine mane
or just become a Superscruff,
a wild man of Melbourne, not Borneo,
with or without a topknot?
A prospect too scary to contemplate
a house without mirrors suddenly appealed.

Stephen Alomes

Milestone Mania

As a newbie grandpa, don't you swell like a nappy-full

when you first hear
Him babble away & just know He'll speak a dozen languages

when you first hear
Him say *ball* or *dog* & think they're distinct physics sounds

when you first hear
Him shout *quack* at a duck & are positive He's Harvard bound

when you first hear
Him shriek *eyes* & decide He'll one day be an ophthalmologist

when you first see
Him nod at *hungry?* & be sure He'll never ever eat junk food

when you first see
Him hit balls & tell He's as gifted as a son of Tiger Woods?

And, as a newbie grandpa, when you see
Him happy to kiss every person in the room, except you

don't you want to rub His cute face in a swollen nappy-full?

Virgil Goncalves

Angelic Beauty

A father but never a parent, I long ago
renounced any right to a relationship with my offspring.
Procreation is simple, paternity complex

and healing sensitivities associated
with renunciation requires tact and toleration
that may or may not be successful.

But I have been blessed: today I heard a
boy-child cry and, holding a grandson
where once was none, gazed in adoration.

No eyes have beheld such angelic beauty!
No thought of the heart so emotionally moving!
The birth of this, or any child, is an epic boon,

proving life is festooned with greater
benefits than self-gratification, the accumulation
of power, pecuniary gain or reputation.

Jeremy Gadd

A Grandson Travels Face Time

his whispers crept across my face
mapping each contour and crevice

this one's deep like a cut
what would have hurt you then
the silk of his hair
blew like rye grass mending

maybe you buried something here
it's lumpy and feels sad
his breath smelled of cherry tree
loveliness

I know when you got married
it made the line all frilly
and he showed me the greenness of
of morning love

this must be when I was born
it's the longest 'cause I made you a grandmother
his finger travelled from my nose bumpily
lifting the fallen corner of my mouth

Elizabeth Goodsir

Gifts from us and beyond

There's a first-time busker in Rundle Mall,
young, beautiful, dressed in Edwardian style,
– straw boater, op shop skirt,
handmade blouse, boots.
She looks the part, and sings
with all the confidence of youth,
self-taught ukulele her accompaniment,
her song carried to the passing crowd
by the amplifier she saved for and bought.

Shoppers pause to stare and smile.
'There's talent,' says one to his wife.
'Yes, dear, she deserves some money.'
Five dollars tumble to her music case.
At closing time there's real generosity:
Twenty dollars, fifty flutter down.
She's amazed when she counts it all.

I'm amazed. She's my granddaughter, just eighteen.
At that milestone, I was shyness itself.
I loved to sing, but played not one note.
Are our children, and theirs, always other
and more than ourselves?
She is her own self.

Dawn Colsey

Marriage Is

marriage is the coldest corner
of winter
is a worm with both ends the same
is the rotting petals that gather
on the windowpane
is a wet animal who enters
the back door
is the rain that falls
like confetti
on the driveway
is a museum of forgotten
memories
is the promises
that run down
dead-end streets
marriage is the last log on the fire

Jules Leigh Koch

Wedding Photo

They wait stock-still
in froufrou dresses –
bouquets held loose
in their arms

humble their presence
without presumptions

Unbreathable quiet
an ultimate hush –
now, long since parted

under wide-brimmed hats
and floating veils –
pale faces stare straight
back or past

or through me

Seated bolt upright
post-dated beside them
three men in black

seeming awkward –
oversize hands poised
gentle on their knees

Darrell Coggins

The Simple Things

Last Saturday night
I cooked dinner
as he, spray in hand,
stalked a fly around my kitchen.
Later, he trimmed my trees,
repaired my hose nozzle,
helped me load the dishwasher.

I remember
other Saturday nights,
when we jived beneath the moon,
did cartwheels in the sand,
read each other love poems.

Next year,
we celebrate
twenty years together.

Kathleen Fernandes

25th Wedding Anniversary

The night my mother left my father he cried all night long –
silent tears slowly dampening his pyjama shorts,
the first sign of vulnerable emotion I'd ever seen.

On the kitchen table her anniversary present sat unopened,
gaudily wrapped like a fat reproach – Arpège again I guessed.
Next to it her goodbye note, scrawled blunt and brief.

A quarter century of marriage, of quiet untogetherness,
an ambivalence of opposites, the long years together
now hanging heavily, like a miscarriage of justice.

Resentment had festered in my mother's virginal heart
since their Victor Harbour honeymoon, playing tennis.
She realised then she'd made a 'terrible mistake'. She hated tennis.

'But I loved her,' sobbed my father while my hand patted his leg.
His statement, a question mark, curling into the ether,
reaching out to hook a now uncertain future.

Cary Hamlyn

A Ruby Anniversary

an easy complicity
a gang of me and you
a wordless felicity
conspiracy of two

a hug with benefits
less urgent   still a spark
time won't wait   let's be spendthrifts
in the maw of the dark

no confessions, repentances
no need to bare the soul
finishing each other's sentences
(forty years   no parole)

John Carey

Our Diamond Wedding...

We've loved and lived and argued now for over sixty years,
togetherness the true cement of laughter, smiles and tears
and as the years of compromise direct the route to take
we cosset with impunity the plans we hope to make.

We travelled many a foreign road; our children met the pace
till school, careers and marriages decreed we halt the race.
They too have stories yet to write, tales they wish to tell
We smile with silent certainty, assured they'll do it well.

For us, another page has turned, a closing one begun.
'The moving finger writes and having writ moves on...'
Centuries old, those words so wise resound upon the page
Reminding us that 'moving on' is commensurate with age.

A rich book lies behind us, more pages beg the seers.
A lifestyle to be scripted well beyond these golden years.
We've reached a milestone now we feel but many years await.
So now, with all who shape our life, it's time to CELEBRATE!

Maureen Mitson

Just Rewards

Living is its own reward, she said:
my atheist mum, who railed at those occasions
where giving gifts was customary. You'd not
deserve a celebration – not for lasting,
nor for any possible achievement.
Decades on, I wonder whether we
rewarded her enough.
                For me, perhaps
reward resides in something like belonging,
something like solidarity:
that someone went before you, cleared a path,
cared you not get lost, toiled to carve
a number in stone, so you can keep believing
in a town's existence as you tramp along
through all weathers in ill-fitting boots.
Someone planted palms along a street,
set out flower beds in a public garden,
wrote a book describing, unflinchingly,
a dying parent's eye, while a full moon rose,
as if reaching back in time to clasp your hand.
Someone built a house that needed care –
new stumps, new roof, new
hearthstones – climbing frames of life
where three loud children flourished.

Carolyn Masel

New Home

2005–2020

Calves bawl for mother. Mothers bellow from nearby paddock

Neighbour's dog barks all day when she's not home

Hoons race in the main street at 3 a.m.

Magpies warble delightfully

Chainsaws roar for winter wood

2020–2021

Hens cluck resoundly next door. Half an hour continuous

Neighbour's terriers yap territorially at our backyard

The cul de sac is blissfully quiet at 3 a.m.

An unknown bird sings delightfully

Leaf blowers roar at autumn leaves

Susan Fitzgerald

Out of the dark…

The weatherboard house is pole-tethered halfway up
the slope of dried grass, summer fires threaten again –
inside, rooms are darkened by towering blue gums
planted with youthful enthusiasm 47 years ago;
swathes of curling bark litter the ground and branches fall,
one killed a koala on a hot and windy Australia Day.
Like the prow of a sailing boat, the back deck rises high:
cockies screech, argue over feeders, white-bomb the floor,
bejewelled lorikeets wait and gossip on the Hills hoist
while magpies in dinner suits eat a smorgasbord below.
Inside, estate agents inspect, evaluate, tap walls, murmur
It's so seventies…so are we, don't want to be fenced in
by 'Good Neighbour' steel, a manicured garden, a house
without character…then, a whisper on the wind,
flat ground, no more mulching bark, no stairs…louder,
no more hard yakka…insistent, *time to smell the roses.*
South we go to hunt houses, some too small, some too big,
we feel like Goldilocks…but now mature roses beckon,
pink out front, glowing gold next to emerald green fernery,
warm apricot on the other side; the house itself is *just right,*
windows frame garden views on three sides, maggies forage,
we move into the light…

Sue Cook

New House After Fire

This new house that I'm living in
is beautiful like a song of joy in clear morning air,
as clean as that, as pure.

I learn to love it as as one loves
in an arranged marriage between good people.
I talk to it. 'Hi House,' I say, and ask it
to care for us and promise to care for it.
I sing into its echoing corners,
promise laughter and love.
I begin the work of that.

I bring objects: plants and feathers, shells and stones.
I place them, like offerings, on the altar that it is.
It begins to feel warm, heart warm,
and cool on hot days,
as welcoming as a shelter,
which, of course, it is.

One day soon, I know,
I will open the silent front door,
heavy, and gliding on its hinges,
and instead of saying, 'Hi House,'
I will say, 'Hello Home.'

Belinda Broughton

at the gatepost

I had asked for the photo –
historic moment, I said
Brother-in-law was eager
to get on the road so
I had to take the photo myself

Two sisters have shut the gate
for the last time, behind us
a childhood of squabbling in the car
about opening and shutting gates
on farms and country roads

The parents dead, the house is sold
the trucks gone, the skip is full,
the cars are filled to legal limits
with remnants of 70 years
from garden, house and shed

We stand at the paddock gate
laughing about our first selfie
We've looped the old chain ring
over the hook that final time
Brother-in-law revs the engine

Jacqueline Buswell

Peace Cottage

Made a successful offer on my 48th birthday
Two bedrooms and a postage-stamp backyard
A vintage rotary clothes line for my children
To swing merrily around on when I'm not looking
Just like I used to in my grandmother's garden.

Lively greenery thriving beneath our silver letterbox
Agapanthus, wiry weeds and wild buffalo grass
Framed by a flaking metal fence and retirement dreams.
A cheery footpath from the iron gate to leaded glass door
Welcomes loved ones to rest a while at Peace Cottage.
Built 1935, barely noticeable to passers-by with busy lives
Cloaked in beige weatherboards and a rusting tin roof.

A makeshift garage squeezed up along the driveway
Sheltering an external laundry beside the kitchen window
Chopped wood for the lounge room fireplace
Stacked in an otherwise empty workshop, full of memories.
My gran used to call her old shed like that a 'lean-to'.
When she reached my age her house had become
A favourite gathering place for family and friends
Gran would have wished the same blessing on my first home.

Gabrielle Journey Jones

Does she feel us as intruders

Does she feel us as intruders
our new old house – our home?
Does she hold the years of generations of love
and living
birth and death as burdens
or a part of her structure to being
is she, in all her imperfections perfectly right and whole
the cracks and stumbles of stone
the paint of fade in time
the little tears of leaks
give her
herself
a grand lady vibrant and living
moving forward with each family
we are not intruders but paths
to a fuller future
we, her, are us
complete

Myra King

Seclusion and Surfacing in Victoria

Curled in our oyster shells, pearls may yet emerge
from the grit. We will fall upon one another,
cast our seeds when summer fades to
autumn. Seclusion is unfolding, when artists
and scholars sought solace in time that stretched
to capture creative flow far from ignoble strife.

I found a world in a grain of sand on the doorstep of
detachment. Feasted my mind on silence in a retreat
free of crippling congestion. Alone, ideas flowed from
an infinity of space on an island split by playfulness and
pain. A place to gaze into spheres uncursed by censure –
or may the solitude make us mad?

Time to fall upon one another, scatter our words
to find that similar souls do not steal time but
enrich its flow into fruition, do not carve creative crops
into poor little pieces but ease and cradle their birth
until they emerge fully formed unto worlds where they
withstand both pummelling and praise peacefully.

Ann Simic

Beer poured on Romeo

London –
A girl who was sacked after tipping beer
over an office Romeo has won
the first tribunal-heard sexual harassment case
under the Sex Discrimination Act.
Townsville Daily Bulletin, 14.9.1983

Beer and breasts don't mix
Poured half a pint, over him, office Romeo, wasted on him,
On all his mates, who think the party is for them,
          a hunting party
Office girl is fair game, they're after breasts and
                    neck, and thighs without consent
Romeo in action, grabbing, prodding, touching, skin
                    crawls under unwanted hands

Hurt doesn't cut it, not really, it's assault in action,
                    full view. Five hundred dollars for
'Feelings'! Understatement, creeping hands need scrubbing
           off, gag-reflex

Sandra Renew

Snaring Grace

no sky

no stars

more like smoky Mars

swirling inflections

of untold reflections

form perception deception

and liminal grief

no next week

no tomorrow

just this moment of reprieve

Mignon Patterson

Inbox

Costly friend,
my name Handa Hamzen is,
and i have a client
investor financial advisor
to invest the wealthy sum
of five million roubles
in profitable adventure capital
in your country under their worry.
very top law policeman
my customer is in his country
you can handle him investments
in your country for a decade time
he will give you 30% of total plant.
recontact me back through
this confident email
also sent your Names, full address,
and PIN number and you will receive
an investment strategy I give you.
Thanking for how i want your respond
and you will achieve
a very great Millstone in your life
with most regards,
Hamza Hamden.

Gordon McPherson

exact coinage

we're lined up (as you do)
on a Saturday,
each with our handful of
six-pack or Cabernet Merlot promise,
mind's full of justify
(it is Saturday, not thinking,
of course, about the
Escher-logic required
for the morrow)

she's in front of me
clutching two cans of Export,
cheeks ruddy and corrugated,
puppet eyelids,
then, at the counter,
a slurry of lips, words, sense
but she's got exact coinage for
her booze and pack of
Winnie Golds, she's got
her night sorted

Kevin Gillam

City Warrior

Bold like the colours of a city
Or is it
Monochrome
Isolating

Can one hide in buildings reaching the sky?

Can one still grow like a tree between concrete?

Time to challenge like an unfaltering warrior
Brave in attempting concepts anew
Brush aside notions of failure and pride
Press forward to new potentials

Barbara Gurney

Salvation

To win or lose the common cause,
against the weight of chance,
can rest upon a moment's pause –
or hasty sidelong glance.

To strive to seek and fail to find,
inside a fallow year,
can whisper ghosts upon the mind –
to fabricate the fear.

And argue with subjective truth,
to beat against the tide,
on quicksand joy of bygone youth –
in sanctuary denied.

We salvage love from pagan hope,
like innocence at play,
and release at last the hangman's rope –
the God we carved from clay.

Ian McFarlane

Reptilian Milestones

What are yours,
squat, determined Aussie
on efficient short legs?

Was it when you hatched
in Anne's garden?
Or the first time
you emerged from among the irises,
answered to the smell of water,
lapped from the fish pond,
wrapped your tongue around
flies, mossies, Anne's kitchen scraps,
ignoring noisy miners and magpies?

Have I understood
some milestones
in a blue tongued lizard's life?

Alice Shore

Grey Honeyeater

Karijini National Park

This small pale species,
its local name given us by Banyjima people,
a grandmother, her granddaughter
wishing luck, smiling.

And finally, the bird
feeding on mistletoe nectar
in the mulga, *Acacia anura.*
We mask our tears with steaming coffee;
grins as wide as the continent.
Our tick-list of all seventy-three
Australian honeyeaters is complete!

Ignoring the wave of Wittenoom ghosts,
the Keep Out signs at iron ore and gold mines,
we'll drive our memories
the five thousand kilometres home
then raise a glass
to the gorge carved through red rock
and the soft chatter of women sharing their *Jirrunypa.*

Jack Oats

Jirrunypa – Aboriginal name for grey honeyeater

First car

Hondas were best, you said.
So I bought a Honda Civic – a hatchback,
automatic, the colour of custard, of capitulation.

You taught me to drive. A friend untaught your teaching.
Drive like that, he said, you'll kill yourself.
Worse. Damage the car.

I loved driving. I threaded my way
through city traffic to my teaching job.
Stitched up the roads en route to Riverland holidays.

Driving got me places you'd never been
to do things you'd never done.
Marry a man you didn't approve of.

You were right about the man,
but a Hyundai Accent – red, manual –
beats a Honda any day.

Louise Nicholas

Nicking Across the Nullarbor

pre-loved caravan hitched with difficulty
I edge my way onto the bitumen   breath
you're doing what   *at your age*
incredulous voices echo in my head

the gods are not kind   heavens open
trusty GPS takes me on a wet clay road
car and caravan slide   my heart thumps
I'm too old to cry   howl *it is not fair*

no longer a touring virgin
I start to enjoy myself
cliff faces   scrub   tall trees and starry nights
etch into my memory

pristine beaches   smelly seals
90 miles of straight road across a treed landscape
red dirt   clear blue skies
space stations in the heavens

8000ks there and back
they say   *you did what*

I smile and lie
    a piece of cake

l.e.berry

Nihonbashi, Edo, 1860

The *furoshiki* wraps my few saved coins,
a *shakuhachi* flute,
balls of rice each with a pickled plum at its centre,
       squeezed and cupped and wrapped in dried seaweed
       by Junbe-e from our Master's household,
       who I will never see again but in feverish half-sleep
a washcloth, an undershirt and extra *waraji* sandals
       should I keep walking when the pair I wear today
       become thin threads
       like those now barely still connecting me
          to this place of employ.

I leave tomorrow before dawn,
first to Nihonbashi,
       not one *ri* away,
       the milestone beginning the five great
          Go-Kaido highways
       where the divine, a new patron, or a whim
       might take me west, or north,
       to where I could entertain travellers
       with music or a strong and willing body.

Derek Baines

Edo – known as Tokyo since 1868

Bluestone Station

They drop you at the platform with
a one-way ticket and a shrug.
You board the hefty Pullman
get shunted off to somewhere's end.
Watch, through air-conditioned, dulled zest
and double-glazed eyes the
clover paddocks flash swiftly by.
Wonky tracks collaborate
trick your sense of north and south.
Point blades switch, scotch your goal
bung you up in a goods train siding.
Prim locos ping ballast sideways
from the shiny main line
gloriously careering to their end.
You watch and wait, watch and wait
night drifts in with its terror of termination.
Then off you go, into the night
where flagmen keep their lanterns lit.

And you arrive, at a bluestone station
stand silent and alone
caught under a moth eaten beam of electric light.
Cloaked in a pilled wool trench
search forlornly for the gate
dragging your body and your baggage to the line.

Jane Carmody

35 M

Hidden among undergrowth
       beside a disused track
this rock, this stone,
       feet firmly planted in its soil
moss covered, top rounded, worn.
       On lichen-encrusted face
etched large: 35 M; almost obliterated.

To Marmion from Mull maybe,
       my map of this land is muted.
And, what of me at thirty-five,
       lurching from one crisis
in Miocene to yet another
       somewhere in the mountains
feet dancing over snow.

Moving back to my flat land
       where rocks are older by far
than this crouching goblin,
       this mysterious milestone.
My weathered land accepts me.
       It knows my mind is
firmly planted in its soil.

Jean McArthur

Fingertips

Fingertips silver-black
grip strings on ebony – it's winter in Madrid

All night: *coñac*, taffeta,
compelling rhythms, hands fast and light…

Midday: Luis teaches another *falseta:*
'*Otra vez, más lento…* ' I get it clumsily down

Gaze from the icy third-floor balcony,
people arm-in-arm in the street below
God it was cold!

Off-season
I could practise in the room if I paid in advance
and after three hours, fingers split and bleeding

But we were young and healed quickly then…
A silk shawl for a girl a lifetime away?
Nothing hurt for long. Guitar smiles back.

Evening: hungry stroll through frozen park by
fading light, fingertips scabbing over

Letter in my pocket says, 'It's time you let go.'

Christopher Nailer

White on Red

'We can meet you in Carennac.'
A Brisbane friend, Moët in hand,
smiles across a tray of hors d'oeuvres,
with creamy Brie and dark tapenade, French treats.

She's aware of my limitations,
my gentle mien, my pallor –
more Jane Austen than Cathy Freeman.

A solo cross country hike,
midsummer France. Mmmm…

But now, STAGE 5. GLUGES TO CARENNAC. 22 km.
Map swings in a plastic wallet, walking poles click.
French nursery rhymes and drinking songs
sound my pace. A red hat and pink face.

TAKE THE GR 46 – I love those white and red blazes.
Past the old abbey and then four hamlets. Hamlet?
Do those four bars mean farm buildings or hamlet?
GR 652 appears – then Floirac, some cross country.
Streams. DANGER! But *voilà!* Carennac!

'Cooee!' Blistered, corned beef feet can't mar my joy.
Insecurities blitzed. Warm Aussie hugs ahead.

Denise Parker

Two Years in Yemen

An unexpected telegram arrived, at a moment in our lives
when the children had left home and we were free
to fulfil a long held dream to help the disadvantaged,
an invitation to teach children of the ancient city of Taiz.
I cannot forget our first impressions:
armed guards slouching beside the school compound gate
high stone walls capped with jagged glass and barbed wire
and our Aussie friends with open arms and beaming faces,
the children, flashing eyes, attention seeking
the boys, bumptious and garrulous
the girls already bending to male domination
children whose boundless energy we learned to harness
who earned our respect and who came to accept our ways,
the women, draped in black and hidden from men's eyes
or confined behind steel gates or high barred windows,
donkeys, small and meek, carrying water casks from the well
or loaded high with firewood and beaten with a stick.
I salute our school principal Saleh, and his deputy Sultana,
whose flaws and faith endeared them and whose dedication
to their little Arab students made the school a happy place.
I learnt to accept the threats and limitations of this
autocratic democratic republic and to live in harmony
with its people. Inshallah, everything would come to pass
as God willed. Little girls converted me to Islam days before
we left, as they could not let me go home unsaved.

jacqui merckenschlager

Dark Dots and Sunshine

At the crest of Lyle Hill, I gasped in wonder at flashing
silver daggers of light dancing on the surface of Holy Loch.
The *Empress of England* sat still on the sacred waters.
Mothers held small hands tight.
Fathers re-counted travel bags. A grandma sobbed,
'Remember me. Fare thee well.'

Fleeting impressions carved Atlantic water into a random
mapwork of fluid borders rising to heights that erased
tears, years and *Thou Shalt Nots* of my Dark Island.
The sight of my homeland settled into furrows.
Humps shrunk to a line on the horizon.
I watched the last dark dot disappear.

The wide Saint Lawrence embraced the *Empress*
to smooth her passage. The maple leaf flag
slapped the wind and seagulls scattered.
Gardens with rainbows of colour said 'hello'.
May sunshine warmed the day.
A voice whispered, 'You are safe. I love you.'

Rose Helen Mitchell

Vivid

The departure has always been blurred – a train trip
to a drab London dock; dark warehouses; grey river
and sky, seeming one. And it's strange that you can't
recall boarding. But you do remember a feeling of awe –
standing on the great ocean liner, looking way down
on a world, suddenly so small. Sepia memories – few
below to wave farewell; no bright streamers tossed high
to clutch till torn apart; only one white, upturned face
of grief. But memories can lie– she wasn't there –
she couldn't bear to come and see her family leave.

All that greyness, receding – grief, nostalgia, travelling
with you over the ocean, tossed up in foam, washed
in the wake, subsiding. Everything moving forward, yet
time, in limbo, as weeks drift by. Until at last, you wake
to a coastal sunrise; arrival day dawns fine and clear.
Years will never change the suspense, held, in that slow
sweep, the stately turn between the Heads as the ship
entered Sydney Harbour. Word spread fast -–all were
up on deck, hanging over railings, dazzled by the light;
straining to watch the pilot taken on board; ferries
crossing, tugboats bossing, hawsers straining, bilges
draining, seabirds falling from an endless blue sky.
Ahead, the Harbour Bridge, entry to a new life. Vivid.

Gillian Telford

Pathways

Another milestone
has been reached today,
refugees out of lockdown
         more hurdles to pass
after surging seas
with nothing to call
home in new lands where seeking
         safe shelter's calm life.
Rites of passage seem
inconsequential
beside harsh hurdles people
face on arriving.
         Compassionate lands
         found wanting this day,
         doors for asylum seekers
         closed, misunderstood.
Another milestone
another story
the wealth of which lies hidden
         beneath grey blankets,
old snow on pathways
sand deserts and stone
border guards, yet fresh faces
         promise hope this time.

Adèle Ogiér Jones

Farewell to number forty-five

In my sleep you are brought down
in a hail of litigation, all the revolutionary ghosts
pouring down their rain dance tap dance
within the spoilt offices of your epiphany.
You are shadow boxing, always one foot ahead
in a spar, looking over your shoulder
for redeemers, basking in the fortitude of rage.

When I wake you are yesterday's news, confounded,
ex this and that but riddled with rumours and silent.

It goes on. In a dream you are exempted on a faultline
of your own devicing – orange, purple, quaffed and sore.
There are like-minded people, and the easily bought,
verbalising in their warped senseless about the
abandonment of their excuses. We wait in a bate of breath
but when I wake again there are still newsreels
that see capital in ongoing sagas.

Nightmares are tied in a spool of long ties, imperial red.
Until, finally, there is a new poem on the Capitol steps.

Helga Jermy

Hell is us!

rebutting Sartre's *#Hellisothers (L'enfer c'est les autres)*

This winter of discontent,
      this pandemic season of hell,
      gives way to a mantle of dazzling light.
Gone are the wretched lockdowns.
Gone are sagging grey skies.

Time for action!
Dining, drinking with friends,
      a show or two. Music!
      drumming and dancing drive us all.
People abound, not one soul's left out.

We witness the clatter of new vigour.
The traffic's disgorging fuel,
      the hazy planes above
      spewing our fumes
      back to us.

We have wasted water,
      we've disavowed the truth of climate change
      we've caused wild bushfires.
Threatening winds and fires are closing in.
Hell is us, not others!

Anne-Marie Smith

And her pale fire she snatches from the sun

(*Timon of Athens*, Act IV, Scene iii)

I have seen   the first   swan neck
of the season   unfurl   above a parapet
of snow   driven by   its genetic engine
ignoring   the vagaries   of extreme weather
unlike the stem   which bent   to my fickle will

The next day   in a cut glass vase   you could see
its virgin shroud   tainted brown

I learned   that a snowdrop   is best left in place
alone   with the mystery   of its swaddled face
perfectly formed   silk-spun cocoon
bowed   by superstition   blood stains
biblical myth   Victorian foreboding

Julie Maclean

A costly legacy

authority is total   the way it's gotta be
  black lives matter   cofveve   how about bleach
   a bad grouping of tornadoes   cast doubt on facts
    about what imperilled   the world's agenda
   how fraud paled   the troika laundromat
  and what's with   turkey's gas for gold
a new variant of virus?

the dirt   scandals   a hand overplayed
  violent   deadly   incompatible with law
   arrogance   racism   antifa done it
    senators forsook   a scene of crime
   shaking heads at   find some votes
  everyone there   saw what happened
the world not there   gasped it happened.

bonnie and clyde   make this go away
  is it constitutional   who's fake news
   but nobody's asking   where the ventilators
    it's pinocchio's nose   dead right it is
   a plan is close   let's go back to the regular
  but a question for scholars   is it just politics
a vote is all it takes   or a secret pardon.

Eugen Bacon

Safe... The Pandemic

Everyone needs order,
clothes rehung,
cut roses secured in
a vase.

When we move,
when we place one foot
and then the other,
we can put small things in place,
an email to a friend in another country,
bags of rubbish carried out
to the bins.

Our brains, wired this way,
want the winter doona
smoothed squarely across the bed,
the freezer stocked, and remotes
in position.

After we get out, we have only to move
cautiously, surrounded by so much space.

Libby Sommer

Lockdown, Melbourne, July 2020

Gone are the drumming feet,
The tangled conversations
And the tidal comings and goings of trams and cars.
Now, in the grey, untidy dusk,
You hear the swish of a skirt,
The anxious stab of high-heel shoes
And, perhaps, a bell cold siren.
Doves still circle the spire of Saint Paul's
And settle among the gargoyles.
But the cranes perched above construction sites
Now hang, grey as desiccated spiders
And the CBD lies, almost deserted.
In a park where children came catapulting,
Butterfly bright in the mornings,
A raven preens its feathers,
Snatches discarded scraps of food, lopes away
And the first month of lockdown shrugs its shoulders,
Steadies to begin the next
And an enemy, too small even to see,
Continues to besiege the city.

Bill Cotter

Herd Immunity

We sought to make the best decision.
We gathered quickly to do our best.
To spread it round became our mission.
Politicians, bureaucrats, a joint vision:
In Covid times we had to save the blessed.
We sought to make the best decision.

Our first proposal brought no division
Between Sir Humphrey, Dan, and all the rest.
To spread it round became our mission.
Blame the Feds? No, that lacked precision,
Sir Humphrey mused, and then professed:
'We are here to make the best decision.'

'A creeping assumption spiced by vision!'
Dan spoke well, and got it off his chest.
'To keep it creepy will be our mission!'
'It lacks deniability, that new position.'
Sir Humphrey now was at his very best.
'A creeping blank is the best decision.'

Yes! His plan to save us was a magic pill.
We were all infected but none were ill.
We sought to make the best decision.
To spread the blame became our mission.

Nicholas Hasluck

Anniversary

A year ago today my world was smashed
by a man in a suit and wire-rimmed glasses.
His voice was small and grew smaller.

Over the next nine months I lost my aversion
to needles and swallowing tablets
found I preferred my hair short.

So I take my husband out to dinner
like some macabre anniversary
because I feel the need to mark this path

from a place that howled to one made of bricks
where I savour the simplest things –
the sharpness of orange juice in the morning

how fast I can cycle with the wind behind me
watching the sun slip into the sea.

J V Birch

to the little one inside me

i know you're scared
i can feel you cry
you're not toxic little girl
this journey's not yours
the chemo's flowing
through adult me
i promise you're safe
it won't be for long

Sue Donnelly

20 September 2018

Today the oldest child of my older child becomes a teenager,
and I become officially older than either of my parents.
My granddaughter and I are heading into uncharted waters.

For her, as the first signs of womanhood emerge,
there are many adventures yet to be lived,
much to experience and learn. She has life-light in her eyes.

For me, it feels like I am into borrowed time,
genetic clock ticking, telomeres fraying.
Despite precarious beginnings it's been a rich, full life.
I should feel blessed and I do. But I am frightened.
Not for myself, but for my younger child.

She's raised her children, earned her degree, just begun
her long awaited career; an emerging chrysalis.

But there's a hairline crack in this family milestone.
She's out of her depth, far too young, battling cancer.
She fights for her allocated three score years and ten.

May we all be given time
for our life stories and our wings to unfold.

Margaret Clark

A Stalled Journey

Years melted away today:
I saw again that first awakening of infant eyes
      decades ago on the road of time.
Not the first, but assuredly you were
a surprising milestone in my life:
the child I was told I never could have.
Sensitive and gifted you drifted
from brilliance to complexity,
travelling from laughter to youthful despair;
a few miles passed while I hauled you back from there.
Maturity was marked by brighter signs
leading to success and shared joy
      until halted by Fate's bitter hand.
Milestones now weighed heavy in my heart;
like stacked hard miniature headstones
they formed barriers to block all progress.

      I have watched you lying in pain,
your journey stalled, the roadmap of your future in shreds.
Then today, for a few brief moments you woke,
dark eyes shining as in infant wonder;
      you smiled
and I saw along the road ahead
future milestones re-spacing, reforming,
      offering hope
          and the answers to prayers.

Dianne Kennedy

Reading in Bed – a Milestone

I can no longer read in bed,
my chiropractor informs me –
no lying cosily ensconced
tome in outstretched hand
swapping sides when neck
and shoulder muscles &
eroding cervical vertebrae
begin to scream their jibes

I try to follow his advice but
sitting propped up in bed
with pillows doesn't cut it
cannot match the fuggy cave
of bed clothes and their subterranean
entry to otherworlds of fancy.

So I purchase a relining sofa
soft cushions and a mohair rug
prop my book against the armrest
and crawl into my pseudo cave
it's not the same but beggars
they tell us can't be choosers
and if wishes were horses beggars
would ride. And so I ride
oh – still I ride.

Terry Whitebeach

The Climb

Five months after the gift
of a bovine heart valve
my body does not feel normal.

Short walks are tough
but I attempt at last
the long-favoured hill climb.

My absence seems to draw rebuke;
each step is cautious
pausing to sense reaction

as the trail winds upwards
under clouds that hide the sun
until at last from veins and sinews

deep and surface mind
joy surges as the body remembers.
This hill remains my friend.

Paul Williamson

Remission

The mind
Creativity and imagination
Unleashed
Involuntary thoughts
Theories of reality
Conceived by humanity
Under examination
Illogical intellect
A jigsaw puzzle jungle
Missing pieces
Confused
Lost
A merciless brain synapsis flow
Constant alarm and collision
Fear, sorrow, anguish
Medication change
Tranquillisers
A manageable crisis
Symptoms recognised
A rational enquiry, investigation
Awareness, insight
Challenging emotions
Peace explored
A different realisation
A breakthrough in transmission.

Jean Winter

Launched

inspired by Cameron Irwin of Clifton Beach, Tasmania

Hazy recollection still, waking bolted into brace.
Of voices quick and sharp; not waves.
Fluorescents, catheter, morphine drip,
Till faces loom into view: nurses', doctor's, mum's.
Her word: 'T-boned'.
Could still put words to thought. 'Everything?'
Tears, tissue: 'You, surfboard, car.'
Smile working too. 'One, two, three in priority.'
And sight. 'I know I'll not walk again, mum.'
Heart kicking: 'But my arms and hands are awesome.'

Sam, quad bike back from out west:
Granville Harbour to the Pieman and back.
Could ride the roughest tracks, so what chance the sea?
Fear spikes, him thinking, staring out at the break.
'Right, let's do this. But I'll need help.'
Lifted, lowered belly to board. Mates surround.
Vinny: 'If he starts to drown,' Scans the dozen,
Sam's mum sitting above them in the sand,
'Grab him by the scruff of the neck and toss him back on.'
Shoved out, mates paddling close, push him into waves.
Biggest hurls him into shore, Sam waving survival.
Half hour, tide dropping. Back on beach.
Vinny: 'Bugalugs here caught the biggest of the day.'
'Biggest of our lives as well,' mum mumbles.

Steve Tolbert

Markers of the journey

Long road trips of childhood,
visits interstate.
Bored, we'd watch the milestones
as they slowly passed.
Journeys seemed interminable,
vistas stretching to far-off horizons.
Today I contemplate their speeding by,
the markers of my life.
School, university, romance –
twenty-firsts, then weddings, christenings –
career, more graduations –
flashing past; each year the calendar
swift turned, then fast discarded.
Now the journey's speeding on
with sequences of deaths and funerals
denoting dwindling years.
That childish cry: 'Are we there yet?'
no longer has a note of promise.
These days the signposts of the journey
come with unwelcome swiftness.
Velocity no more a virtue,
no more at our volition.
Now I survey my treasure, milestones of old days,
so fugitive, my only wish to slow their passing,
horizon now in sight.

Valerie Volk

Clean Lines

No one said, no one foretold,
that these double-digit anniversaries
met by thinning hair and aching knees
would be a time of paring back.
Of faces disappearing – never to return.
Of quiet unpeopled afternoons
no words carried on the empty air
and even the tunes of these reproachful piano keys
played as much by muscle memory and intuition
as learning. Pared back lives
with no deadlines or traffic hassles,
no emergencies, just the gentle chiselling
of inconsequential things.
Other brutal losses, keenly felt.
A chunk of stone in the chest for a moment, then put aside
like white dust swept tidily away
…until the pale elegant nude,
polished by pain, stroked
by the shaking hand of the sculptor one last time
…caressed, robed in folds
of cold unadorned marble, is revealed
in these clean lines of love.

Julie Thorndyke

clouds

a truant child saunters autumn streets
cloud-gazes to Whittington – his pockets
bulge with carrots & a turnip – he allows
the bay-mare to nibble his coat, then reveals
the treat – their little game, the mare snorts

a young man plumbs the depths of dreams
of memory, days of wind & rain – damp
unsettled chickens cluck & scratch, a pony
discombobulated, prances the paddock

an older man learns to walk about the clouds
read to the wrens – makes friends with
his absent father – he finds acceptance
a healing balm when dreams call him back
once in the changing light, he caught himself
imagining, what it might have been like for him.

Fraser Mackay

Eleven Pillars

You are one cell meeting another
You are small, vague, unknown; a possible promise
You are slippery, raw, sweat, flesh and blood
You are a fragile beauty in your mother's arms
You are a careful boy with too many cares
You are somehow guilty and innocent both

You are growing hair on your chest
And muscles over your heart
You are ready to stand your ground
You stand it; beating heart and shaking hands
You feel alone in the big world
You are proud and look over horizons

You are able to love, now
Your fierce loves flow like rivers
You have a child, now
A fragile beauty in your arms; no words
You are at home in the world
You elevate and bind and nurture

You are dancing with the world soul
You are far from the surface of life
You are watching your last moon rise
You are dead, you are alive.

Leo Lazarus

Tuned-out

The silence, if God does not bleed any more.

The Creator of thirty years
opportunities
tuned-out.

Meskhenet
Chimalma
Mama Ocllo
Parvati
Kisshōten
Brigid
Damara
Freyja
Aphrodite

I am now
little, lilting Deity
since menopause.

Melinda Jane

Eureka

Eureka! That milestone moment of success.
Top of the ladder, you have made it
Fold your arms in a caress
Share your moment, celebrate
Long day's journey into night
May blessed memories enfold you
And ever more the sun shine bright.

Nance Cookson

Bloom

You were such a stunner, they say
          looking through old photographs.
She didn't know it then. Now she avoids
the camera's unforgiving eye,
              the mirror's gaze.
The face once almond-pale
        is crumpled parchment
the contours of an old map.

The years folding around her
          bring winter wars, where sound
is frozen, the telltale creak
          of tree limbs, glimmers of ice
in a bare landscape.
Each death is your own death,
        each tally yours to come,
its shadow dogs you
          like greyhounds of the hunt.

When sunlight again warms the ground,
          brings forth new foliage,
what might she not give
          to pluck the berries of eternal spring.

Margaret Bradstock

A Curved Legacy

(on turning 50)

My eyes smile through fine lines
tissue thin and intractable
vibrant and myopic
this is how old friends know it is me

My dimples are no longer cute
they sit smugly on my thighs
flabby skin begs to settle in
lines that scream of teenage cries

An Aegean island within
broad shoulders and sunshine
could have been on the Olympic team
I tread water but cannot swim

Shaped like sweet summer fruit
a round belly and supple hips
overripe and juicy
sugary syrup drips from my lips

Redeemed by long lean fingerss
nail beds perfect for polish
my mother's legacy lingers

Mary Chydiriotis

Fiftieth birthday stocktake sale

One comfortable and complete dried skin
A golden age of blood and kin

Home cooking, without a book
Humour to fill the void, an oblique outlook

Looking increasingly between the stars
Constellations of scars

One ego (some minor wear and tear)
Between the future and the past, halfway there

Flirting with exercise, careers that cauterise
A slayer of scorpionflies

A triumph of effort over success
Quiet subversiveness, accumulated people-sense

Of the heart, a fully certified organ donor
Contact the owner

Christopher Palmer

Solo Celebrations

My birthday is a secret,
Friends would make a fuss,
Yet I have marked the milestones
Since I was thirty-plus.

The ruby birthday came along,
I needed cheering fast,
So took a flight on Concorde –
A memory made to last.

When my golden birthday loomed,
I wanted something rare
And chose a trip to China,
A change of cultural air.

The diamond birthday fantasy
Was South Pacific charms,
I found my island paradise
Beneath Samoa's palms.

Jill Nevile

Slipstream

for Stephen and Brenda

My ship like yours, has voyaged long years
upon an effervescent ocean
                        a world of illusions, where
time's perceptions flow, from 'then' to 'now'

Scientists know better than to chart
their course through past, present and onwards

Remembering life's chronology, sometimes
so do I   events intermingle
            was my child's first tooth before or after the
            change of residence, my new work

When was that momentous move and the
'chance' meeting which fills a lifetime?

Gazing in reverse on three score
years and ten, does it matter, if
memory changes sequence?

Jen Gibson

Kilometrestones

I try valiantly not to like cheese
the doc says I have to cut it out
she who surveils the fridge
says you've been at it again
not going to buy it any more
there's never any left when I want a bit

two months to the day I hit 70
that many orbits of the sun
some get on the ride earlier than others
another milestone clocked up
why the heck isn't it metric now?
you know – multiply by 8 divide by 5

it's the calcium that does you
atomic number 20 – alkaline earth element
but this metal warding off little fractures
is secretly building stones
my fourth is at critical mass as I write
and hell it's no picnic shoving one out

70 years eh?
and another gallstone passed

John Blackhawk

My 75 Year Milestone

My milestone is not solitary.
Instead a cairn, built from many.
Ancestral milestones at the base
Supporting the new, as our family grows.
Strengthened by bonds that can't be broken.
Built by the shared experiences of life.
Washed by the sadness of tears.
Warmed by the sunshine of joy.
Rough edges are the sum of us –
Our talents, traits, ideas, beliefs,
All different but entwined with love.
Each stone accepting the other,
Supporting the communal weight
Of happenings past, but not forgotten.
Memories of triumph and loved experiences,
All building my precious family of milestones
Into a cairn.

Marilyn Revill

The Journey

From the marble and granite milestones
marking roads in Britain since Roman times
I flew in 1968 across the world
with my husband and young children.
My first flight, a milestone in itself,
bringing me to a new life in Australia
rejoicing with my parents and grandmother
who had settled six months earlier.
Here, wide-open roads stretched for miles
stand-alone houses – no joins at the seams.
Gum tree-lined streets replaced oaks and silver birches.
Milestones measured the passing years
flashing past as quickly as the markers
we passed on our travels in Europe.
A divorce, a new marriage, a new daughter.
Our own house between trees in the Adelaide Hills,
a koala or two, possums at night and once,
a kangaroo hopped past my window.
Warped pottery and uneven weaving gained me
an arts diploma at college as a mature aged student.
Three beautiful grandchildren
and much laughter before another divorce.
Surviving renal cancer gave me more years
and as my 80th birthday approaches fast
who knows how many more milestones lie in wait.

Jill Gower

Reaching 80

I swung in the trees
and slid down the breeze

I danced in the valleys
and lay in the lees
I sang the lark's song
among anemones

I climbed through those mountains
those cliffs sharp and sheer
searching for footholds
showered with tears

To reach those far fields
to taste that sweet breeze
beneath endless blue
in silence and peace

This was my journey
My landscape my place
An image a dream
Ephemeral space

Maureen Mendelowitz

Some Stones Too Heavy

swimming
my first and lasting
liberation
Dad's patient coaching
in Coogee's ocean pool

playing
netball, tennis, squash
never strongly
somehow keeping up…
lively school and uni years

the joys
of cradling babies
carrying kids
in moves round the world
such a rich life

these arms
paralysed by polio
in '45,
rehabilitated
now support me in old age

Amelia Fielden

A Thousand Paces

I wander down the years to reminisce
on milestones hid in grass and wayside weed,
the crossroads where my judgement was amiss,
when paths I took were falsely based on greed.

I planned each inch of life; the choices made
are measured now in feet that soldier on.
The milestone triumphs scored, how soon they fade,
when set against the joys that were foregone.

Now, as I march towards my thousandth month,
my shoulders bend with millstone might-have-beens,
I leave it to my children to confront
this world of dotty comms and backlit screens

whilst I devise mendacious lines of verse
behind a mask – lest I go viral first.

Tony Fawcus

Milestone

This book in my hand
with its pick-me-up cover
belongs to me. I wrote it.
In other hands it was nurtured
beyond my expectations
returned to me in my 88th year
like an edible feast.

Declared a winner.

Mary Jenkins

Continuities

We put our faith in such occasions so today
I'll bake a cake for you, a Persian love cake.
You're no longer here of course
but even then we'll still celebrate
and remember your thoughtful heart.

Nine candles will stand for nine decades
since you were born and my cake
will be a homely reminder, a symbol
of love and gratitude partnered with laughter.

Years pass and images of candles linger
in my mind, the scented smoke unfurling,
each a living light fixed in thought
as if to provide answers
long after the flames have gone out.

Elaine Barker

The Matriarch

well which footsteps will we
follow – those tiny toe prints, the bawling babe or
the slow shuffle of the 90-year-old matriarch
who followed her gut – called by the sparrow,
the rush of the sea, the echo of song, the silence of stars,
to relish the days stalking goals striding the trails
winding or straight, mile upon mile making the
journey: rainbows came hailstones blundered once
a stylish carriage sadly the hellish marriage
but then maybe we can ponder on me that babe –
'in the beginning…' let me see   yes   once I won
the egg and spoon race – eight years old
in primary, then turning ten was the day when –
ah when? I skipped class, cops found snivelling me
under that bridge, a rickety bridge I must cross to
waken my senses, go with the green light, find
the mystery to make my heart beat with hope, leading
to the first step that would take me to the top
of the stairs – matching the march of the matriarch
                              now, blessed dame, I see
a marker still beckoning at the end of the road:
the Odyssey is almost over, the destination
within reach, nearer nearer it comes, that last milestone
my greatest achievement – if I hang in there
I'll make it

Millicent Jones

End of Visiting Hours

In memoriam Joan Mary Miller

Each visit found you deeper
in the vault of years,
there was no switch I could find
to light my way down the unlit stairs,
only a clumsy fumbling after names,
after memories.
Mostly, I'd find you dozing
or staring in your chair,
the TV blaring in the background.
You'd tell me you're going home,
home to a house that had to be sold
to care for you there.
I'll walk out if they won't let me,
though by then you couldn't even walk
unaided to the foyer.
I'd reach for your hand and kiss your cheek,
I'd place a cushion behind your back.
Not wanting me to go, you'd cling to my arm
as if I were the parent
and you the child.
Before I'd leave, you'd settle again
into blankness,
an uncomfortable silence –
I, too, feared the end of those visiting hours.

Mark Miller

Quiet Grit

He never wore endearments well
those arcane handshakes bared in old dusty cells
where barons of industry guard the shrine
praying for heroes who'd toe the blatant line:
and those heavy plaques bear too many youthful names
who carry forever the eternal flame:
they're sweet flowers laid out on proclaimed days
with scent of glory and scent of death
rusted to steely copper and tarnished brass –
Nay he chose bush-track-heath and empty place
his wanderlust honed with gentle pace:
and his duty is served, and it was hell
though that hero status never sat well –
No he's not for fundraising nor knocking on government doors
he knows corruption and heroes who stand too close,
so he chose quiet walks of unmapped miles
meeting life's weight to cut his style –
and he arrives and leaves without hellos and no regrets
yet his grit and range bear no hidden fear nor defence
for his milestones shine beneath night sky and moonlit tear:
then from dawn and from dusk without a shadow called fame,
his milestones and quiet grit are one and the same!

David Taylor

Your Last Mosaic: Elegy for Eve

You can't pucker your lips to kiss him goodbye.
You cry, and try to apologise
as they wheel you through the theatre door.
'It's all right,' he cries after you, 'you can kiss me
when you wake.'

Twenty years ago, your body was assaulted
with surgery, radiation, chemotherapy.
'Your cancer's gone,' they said, 'but the treatment
has left its mark. It will return in twenty years.'
And so, you waited for your fortieth birthday,
watching always, in vivid life, for death's shadow.

He loves you beyond death. 'I wanted another
twenty years with you,' you whisper.
'Twenty years for us have been like forty,' he replies,
kissing your pale eyelids.

This morning he walks the beach, picking up shells.
Your beach, where you walk and swim at dawn
together.

Your hands are still now. The shells will lie
beside your last mosaic
                    unfinished…

Christina Marigold Houen

A room fallen asleep

im Eugenio Montale

Outside the snowflakes swirl
Toward another destiny
Here no longer
Does a poet's shadow attempt
To fit. Where is the wearer?
The former maker of this fading outline?

Is the soul a tenant
Now flown, to perch
Once more in a new dwelling?
The glass beside the bed
Is empty, the dose of life, since swallowed?

Silence is this brimming emptiness
Once fullness of time. Will someone weep
When stumbling in and they discover
All these sleeping things?

Everything in this room
That served a purpose
Is mute, nothing belongs
Only the last light lovingly clings

And forgotten in a corner; a candle sobbing shadows.

Luke Whitington

Lineage

This is the end that claims us
father to son then father to son.
I walk empty-handed from the mountain
having thrown off the chains of childhood.
Life no longer a quirkish game, there are rules to endure.
Our bond cries out in the echoing voices
of the old ways, the unchanging hymn.
It thrums down the lineage harmonic and resonant
clasping each year with a thin hand of hope.
What a nightmare death becomes –
a coating of mercury, the weight of a stone
a head encased in a mist of toxins.
We collapse under the strain of our own uncertainty.
Shall we pursue or shall we endure?
The binding ties are too young to know.
The milestones we passed are too old.
I shall not awaken the darkest hour.
Let the darkness in our lives have that honour.
I shall not hear the mountain speak your name
for no longer can a child respond.
No longer can a son stand before his father
head bowed, reciting that he understands.
Life is the nightmare; there is no understanding.
We step forward, each of us, into our new skins.

Mark Willing

Climbing Everest, my way

The final ascent is jam-packed, waiting.
Is it ego, glory, grit, a badge of honour?

Some stumbled over frozen corpses,
shuffling past death to reach the summit.
The ultimate experience wooes and beckons.

At Riverglades, I daily meet the challenge:
totting up elevations walked
breathing in loads of life-saving oxygen
hat and fly-screen protected
noting my fitness ever-improving.
Everest – 8,849 virtual metres;
I'll embrace her in a series of mini climbs.

I reflect on accumulated mountain trash,
yawning crevasses of fear,
loved ones left dying near the summit
to save myself and persuasive sherpas.

I conclude that my virtual goal
makes more sense
than the real thing.

max merckenschlager

A Drive Past

The house looks smart now
garage turned into master suite
windows looking onto road
                    garden neat out front
                    grassed and freshly mown
I'm told there is a pool at back
with barbecue and trampoline
family necessities it seems
                    but I remember a different place
when tall gum stood front and rear
and hens scratched dirt
in jacaranda's dappled light
                    I can hear their mutterings even now
                    squawking when an egg was laid
I can see my husband staking beans
or paint brush fertilising passion flowers
piling nature's bounty by the kitchen sink
                    our outdoor room once housed a bat
                    cockatoo Augusta came each day
there must have been grey days of rain
but I remember only sun, the whole place bathed
in warmth when joyful chaos was our chosen way.

Joanne van Kool

bell barred

it takes
precision
for an athlete lifter
to raise
those Olympic weights
into
gold medal position
and so
i stop
think to my life's achievement
and accept

I have done all I could

Geoffrey Aitken

Cartography

How did I come here? How did I find a way?
Those clean and finely contoured maps
I followed in the morning, faded under midday suns.

Much of what and where and who I visited
Was unexpected. That man I saw ahead not he
Who I've become. Midway, I made my dreams my barge

And found myself on shores of inner worlds,
With silence, science and poems my guides.
Making marks upon time's sands (like Birnam Wood)

The impenetrable wilderness has come to me.
The beauty of images is found in front of things;
The beauty of ideas, behind. Moon replaces sun.

Maurice Whelan

roadblocks to recovery were signposts on the way

at fifteen leave school   seventeen go nursing at RPAH
upset fierce army sisters by my shared bed with nurse-lover
smash my leg at nineteen in road crash   work is scarce
for an ingénue from drama school scarred with a limp
in-valid years   a time of mental illness   drugs   alcohol
of AIDS   deaths   when revolution still seemed possible
played stages   theatrical / political – 'a happening'
toured on a rambling bus the Queensland countryside
performed in high schools   comedy   drama   poetry
at Flinders studied Black Theatre stoned on too much LSD
acted in the Ustinov play 'Halfway Up the Tree'
then threw my life away   the time had come to stop
she said 'stay'   I borrowed the airfare and left without delay
my 'wife' took another lover   young student whom she taught
retreat to the bush   water surrounds rocks where eagles soar
admission to Psych Centre   pills and weed mixed with grog
move back to Sydney meet poets   Brown Burns and Viidikas
who write and publish words   to excite   to overthrow
with SUDS act in *The Crucible* and *Bartholomew Fair*
spend seven years in Darlinghurst squat in poverty and pain
write fuming page-spatters to express simmering rage within
sober-clean   bit out of place at the bottom of steep hill
difficult to climb   grow stronger   too sick to go far
play with words   mouthed with a hungry tongue

Jenni Nixon

160

Anniversary tree

J.T. 1924–2003
'Sweet is pleasure after pain' – John Ogden

Through the french doors
a flame of gold
the leaves will fall
this is not death

hiatus

then the nascent buds
bracing to burst
a flurry of white
in spring.

Betty McKenzie-Tubb

cherishing the moments

the thing is…
time has the stealth of a quiet mouse
only droppings evidence of its passing

the trouble is…
time will not be caught nor tamed
as with the joy of friendship
we never know with each farewell
that it isn't the last
for time will not bestow encores
nor linger for our pleasure

the blessing is …
it gives us each moments
to enjoy

the problem is…
it comes without warning
and is gone
only memories evidence of its passing

Colleen Keating

del tempo felice

Hummel. Johann Nepomuk. Trumpet Concerto in E flat major.
Your cheeks puffed out. Still hard to blow your own trumpet
in the kitchen before toast. You were toast at the rehearsal.
Unable to breathe in or out with a sore throat.
Remember that time? So happy in front of a daughter's
wonderment. The practice noise chiming with
the music of the kitchen, cutlery, the sizzling pan, the tap
full on and voices shooting instructions. Everything
in the colour of a business day. You stopped to make music.
Happy tempo from a happy time.

Avril Bradley

A box of photos

without this box of photos
faded, wrinkled, worn

how could I recall the years' acceleration
of signposts blurring past?

my early arm around my grandma's neck
her hat of straw and flowers, askance

– till now my selfied face
with greying hair and skin like hers

many moments exposed to light and time
revealed by whim and wish and love

so what of milestones unrecorded
mislaid round corners of memories' fickle

and all those hands that held the camera too
slipped away down other paths and roads?

no wonder how we clutch these pasts,
precious jewels, fleeing lives
consumed by fire and love

John Bartlett

Awakening Mind

Cut, take two; memories rebooting –
fauna, flora & fragmented lores.

It was back to the cave; embers
at first like restarting the fire.

I felt muscles tic, signals mix up
in fits & starts; recharging again.

I nearly died, but you go on.

Dented body, strong heart with new aims;
other roads to learning, living & being.

Evolving paths, emerging turnstiles –
reframing goals, rerouting milestones.

I learn from people, places, interactions.
I share ideas, music, whatever moves me;

lyrics, images, stories, scudding skies,
nature's memorable moments.

Happiness swells in myriad ways as
practice, purpose & wisdom rebuild.

Jayne Linke

The end of a day

I am walking along a bush path
meditating. Meditating about my life
meditating   in the midst
of a stumble   that sends me stumbling
over a large stone.
You catch my arm
and I continue meditating,
about our lives   together
the milestones in the life   we have shared
calibrated through the mesh
and the mist of memory
as we walk.

Milestones weigh
heavily on my mind
as I sit watching   the sun on the grass
through the blind.
Too many to count, to calibrate
so I leave them to gather – respectfully
on the desk in the room
the sun waiting   on the blind.

Sonia Hunt

Yay!

I was born in a war
on the day Auschwitz began
then bombed out of our house;
how did those milestones define me?

I followed my mother, a survivor,
different roads, different signs
and not usually taking the easy way:
my grandfather, in the first war
fallen, between two ships, into the cold Atlantic,
the uninjured engineer to fix a damaged engine –
he saw the signs, Death, Life – took Death
and on the way went past my grandmother's window –
she said, No, not that way,
so he turned, grabbed Life…
I've made a few mis-steps but I've been lucky and now
my doctor holds two signs, operation and maybe six
or seven years; no operation, maybe two –
I'm choosing the latter and making
Whoopee!

Jacqueline Lonsdale Cuerton

What Can I Say

Silent and solemn they wait for me to speak
I pause as a flood of memories flash by
In the shed my father is making a billy cart
listening to the radio talking about war
Hands shaking a red-faced young boy
is pinning an orchid to my blue taffeta dress
In a valedictory school book is the inscription
'Be good sweet maid and let who will be clever'
Ironing in a gingham apron my baby in a cot
television blaring as a man stands on the moon.
Head high marching defiantly up Swanston Street
behind a home-made banner reading End the War
A market in Marrakesh, a temple in Japan, at Uluru
bewildered by our sins of omission and injustice
In black hearing voices say Sorry for your loss
returning to the vast silence of an empty house
The sound of tiny feet racing down the hallway
shouting Hurry! Grannie's here! Grannie's here!
Courage in harsh times full of bad news and fear
so many acts of kindness from family and friends
At this generous celebration your glasses raised
what can I say? There were so many milestones.

Susie Anderson

Courage

You fell apart back then. It was a serious fall.

Unlike Humpty Dumpty
There were no king's horses,
No king's men, to put you back together again.

You became a rough fragmented whole
That covered a void.
A broken shell.
A hollowed dome.
A bell, with a cracked sound.

Today your work is done.
And you leave with a childhood friend.
Called courage.

You have found a way through.
Over the fence across the meadow.
And into the woods, where the falcons roam.

Catharine Steinberg

Just One Moment Longer

Consider us: this paradox of opposites
called human.
Our songs are rainbow or ash
laughter or lament
our movements shifty as desert dunes.
We speed, slow down
hear distant, near
see microscopic, telescopic.

The brain a storehouse of memory
impulses cruel, kind
betrayals, truths
guilt, innocence
greed, sacrifice.

Though locked in the world's confusions
the taking, the giving
the discontent of choice
we summon angels to stare the devils down
as we watch our loved ones die
wanting them, for just one moment longer
to touch the power – and the urgency of living.

Wendell Watt

To the Bell

The bell is ringing in the street again
And their sons bring them in sleek black Beemers
That they park with the ease of those
Who have the keys to the kingdom now

Forty, fifty years before the bell had rung for weddings
And they had come in battered Valiants and Fords
Symbols of the new life – centrepiece of photos
Back to Rhodos, Sifnos or Athinas
Now melancholy in a shed with dust

In little groups they move toward the tolling bell
The little one ahead shows she knows the way
Old one with a hand on the shoulder of his wife
A golden band, a handkerchief

The crowd swells around the trestle of the fruit man
Eggplant and zucchini, fresh herbs, a dozen eggs
Then they move inside
The low voice of the priest begins to sing
The fruit man's nostrils twitch at the incense
His hour of waiting
An aureole of peace upon him
In the sun
The bell at last is silent.

Robert Horne

Reaching the Line

Are steps I take
preordained to meet a certain length,
my joints their sum of bends,
a point when arms will not respond
and legs refuse to walk.

Do lungs have numbered breaths,
my heart unwinding like a spring
until the coil goes slack,
has pain allotted depth
or love its finite range.

Is there a mark
where all my thoughts will stop,
will I be cast from self
to drift like talcum orchid seeds
and seek another term.

Michele Fermanis-Winward

Stones

They lie
placid and silent, compliant,
weathering storms,
human interference.
A quiet place, the cemetery,
neighbours side by side,
unrelated in life,
connected irrevocably
in death and relegated
to the level playing field
at the end of town.

Silent markers all
of journeys and events,
they bear witness
eternally.

Margo Poirier

The Final Milestone

we have no choice but to face death
time stops
we grieve   we rage   we are in disbelief

there is an empty physical place
where once our loved one stood
a dark well churns within   we surrender

we travel death's circumference
its length, breadth, width   dive deep into its core
drift upon a sea of sensibilities and longing

we surface wiser   stronger
soft beats of our heart
sustain us for what we know shall come

we have no choice but to face death

Thérèse Corfiatis

Cutting: haiku on grief

1. she was born, still

language can not speak
promise drained a valley dry
love is all, is left

2. done

promise knot untied
one becomes two becomes frayed
beginning to end

3. undone

her ribbon sachets
a samba with Ease; his, Guilt
tangles with Promise

Sarah Agnew

Did Not Finish

Lawn half-mown, his glasses on the coffee table
beside an open book
when the ambos came.

> He lived fast, on a steep heel,
> sails taut, the skiff's bow knife-sharp.
> He steered a true course.
> Hand on helm he rounded every mark,
> ducked under the boom as he tacked,
> flung his body out from the gunwale,
> while the wind sang in his ears.
> He thought he could win this race.

> After a turn for the worse, he stalled,
> mast upright, sails deflated.
> Not a breath of wind.

Diagnosis pneumonia, not Covid.
On a ventilator, intubated, an induced coma.
Only one visitor in ICU, his young wife in PPE.

Doctors frantic. CPR. Nothing.
Nothing
would get him closer to the finishing line.

Pippa Kay

The Journey

My mother has died.
She didn't 'curl up her toes' or 'pass away' peacefully.
She didn't 'slip away' and she wasn't 'lost'.
And despite her always telling me that she wanted out
When crunch time came
she fought, clawed and resisted.
If it's all about the journey, then her trip was horrendous.
Struggling for breath, unable to make herself understood
Exhausted, in pain, determined to get out of her bed
Agitated, bewildered, despairing.
After anti-nausea medication, anti-agitation drugs,
painkillers and calmatives were administered
And she suffered the indignity of a catheter
And people prodding and checking and moving her,
She was still on her journey, wanting the world to stop
But not being able to get off.
Finally she succumbed with five short, shallow breaths
Finished, unreachable, gone,
Leaving me standing by the chaotic roadside of her life.
My millstone is her sadness, loneliness, depression.
My milestone is to navigate my disbelief, my what-ifs,
my did-I-do-enoughs,
my guilt.
And to try to make sense of it all.

Diana Harley

Jocelyn

7/12/2020

Our friendship crept up on us, fuelled
by common interests.
Broadening as deeper threads were forged
in shared beliefs.
For years it gently burgeoned unbeknownst to me.
Lives unlike, yet values indivisible.

Later, radiotherapy, then chemotherapy,
became her world.
Courage in every move and grace in every painful step.
One lunch, as we talked of books and food
and wellness, her face assumed a chalky pallor.
At last, she asked for a photo, she'd brought her camera.
Her sister busily arranged us.

Last year she rallied. We talked of loss, the death
of my mother, how she, my work and my purpose
all slipped my grasp, and grief became
a constant shadow.
Yet strengthened as always by Jocelyn's resilience
I survived. We cried, we laughed together.
Yesterday I lost a friend.

Mandy Toczek McPeake

Indigo

Ten years too long
and an absence acute.

I miss your kiss,
the sweet solace of skin;
sleep.

I resent the age of others
and covet the banter of friends.

I envy the ease of lovers.

A lifetime done in the blink of an eye.
I cross my heart and hope to die.
Through a surge of shadow to immerse in light
and nobody knows the dark turns of my mind.

No matter.

I'll be here tomorrow,
a study in survival,
a testament to perpetual motion
and flanked by three saving graces.

You were right, you know, about the sea.

Adrienne Cosgrave

two hearts

for 'pling

my heart beats
way too loud
breathing short & fast
waking at midnight
from deepest sleep

my heart beats
discordantly
i remember dr liz saying
a little arrhythmia
occasionally, is normal – fine

my heart beats
remembering plan e
your saying it's time
to ring dr who

                    gentle zen smile

time travelled
too fast
even for dr who
no generator
reached you

28 november 2018
i wake, custodian
of your quiet heart

kathleen bleakley

When Paris Killed You

for Mehmet

On the early morning you died, at the peak of summer,
Paris pulled out your young heart and
drained it of its last golden pump.
All without consent, and no petals across your lips.
No benevolent guillotine would honour our future now.
The ravenous state spirited you away from me.
Your tired being and love-drenched soul now
immolated beyond the oils and troubled rooftops.
And our pigeons brought the news.
Featherless, their beaks were sealed,
busy, yet, they sat, stunned.
They still do. Your window, a shrine.
My hollowed-out bones are scrimshawed with
rage-filled question marks. I walked cold-blooded
the day we tried to reach you. By nightfall,
your last words were immortalised on screen,
ethereal, love-filled, final.
So, we wake like punctured vessels in this new world now.
Masked, empty, carved. SILENT. The silence…
Our birds, unsure, tiptoe across stony grandiosity
built upon the backs of babes, slaves, you, me –
the intangible hands of power, indiscriminate.
We are left to drip-feed the tear-dried plots
in lands where water is held for ransom and
human flesh is no longer an earthly currency.

Michelle Gaddes

It is Odd

It is odd, the manner they drift away,
in sudden late leaves falling, the onset of spring
full of wattles' exuberance
faint scents of blossom, a hint of daphne
slight on the breeze that becomes shallow breaths
laboured enough to confuse memories,
black and white as *I Love Lucy*,
or sepia cards dealt from the family,
sisters at the beach, one with curls,
Mother in a hat beside a long-suffering donkey
(is there another sort?),
Father in belted uniform,
all that is left between that snatch of life
and the faint howl of mortality
lies in my hands, and her recollections.

Peter Hansen

To the Last Milestone

The last milestone
on a serpentine life road
holds yet
though shadow-loomed
a time eroded
yet still clear inscription
at the interception
of love's interface between
time, eternity,
and a faithful fraternity

knowing...
a harvest sewn to be more
than memory's load,
perceptions' goad
or the balance point of truth
perceived
and received
when the milestone of love
anticipates
ending as beginning, both
and one.

Adrian Rogers

Journey's end

I search for roadside milestones,
those squat sandstone blocks
carved with numbers and letters,
often obscured, yet always there.

Life winds me through a labyrinth,
an array of options, paths that flow
until the ultimate choice beckons,
with no compass to guide my way.

Those milestones now overgrown, lost
at the crossroad, my life half spent as
portents pull me to head-land or heart-land,
to think or feel, or just fade away.

Weary, I crave to rest, claim my grave
convulse, then shiver
with no more breath or beat
at the final milestone my body lies rigid.

My soul wakes and hovers above,
a moonbeam shines upon etched stone,
an increment of earthly time
infused with joy at journey's end,
words clear-cut. It was my tombstone.

Liz Newton

Local Becoming

When my body is so heavy
with transition, another milestone
another transformation, I come to you.

You plural, royal you
collective like my biome
gorgeous bacteria, teeming with life
not greedy with desire
and self-awareness.

Inhale, ingest, remember that I belong
to this space, this present
in every space, close my eyes and listen.

The air is full of birdsong
whip bird, parrot screech, lyrebird, kurrawong
ground in motion with insects, mycelium
mushroom, small violet flowers, prehistoric ferns
the scent of eucalyptus, loam, peat
my hands on a rock, rock lilies at my feet.

Forms change, phase change, the pain will pass
my body will pass, enriching this soil
with organic material. Memory to dust motes
and I will continue to belong in this space.

Magdalena Ball

Alphabet

To contemplate the magic of the word upon the page,
the A to Z of travelling the signposts of a life,
encapsulate the moment in the elegance of type,
the fleeting nature of a life set in the permanence of print,
and as Z approaches, no time to rest on laurels,
yet anticipate the power of the last words in the book.

Rosalind Flatman